FUN DEVOTIONS FOR PARENTS AND TEENAGERS

By James Kochenburger

Family Tree™

Group Publishing
Loveland, Colorado

DEDICATION

It would be inappropriate for me to dedicate this to anyone other than my wife, Karen. Her constant love, patience and understanding have released me to effectively serve in the ministry the Lord has called me to. Without her loving support and encouragement I could not have written this book, nor could I be the father and husband I am today. I owe her my eternal thanks.

Fun Devotions for Parents and Teenagers
Copyright © 1990 by James Kochenburger

Second Printing, 1990

Credits
Edited by Michael D. Warden
Cover and book designed by Judy Atwood Bienick

Scripture quotations are from the Holy Bible, New International Version. Copyright © 1973, 1978, 1984 International Bible Society. Used by permission of Zondervan Bible Publishers.

Library of Congress Cataloging-in-Publication Data
Kochenburger, James, 1962-
   Fun devotions for parents and teenagers / by James Kochenburger.
     p.   cm.
   ISBN 1-55945-016-9
   1. Family—Prayer-books and devotions—English. 2. Teenagers-Prayer-books and devotions—English. 3. Devotional calendars.
   I. Title.
BV255.K63 1990
249—dc20   89-48217
                                       CIP

Printed in the United States of America

ACKNOWLEDGMENTS

No man is an island. And the fruit of a man's life is born out of the rich soil of many close relationships. I'd like to recognize some of those people who have shaped my life and, therefore, the writing of this book:

● To my parents, John and Patricia Kochenburger. You gave me life and have loved me deeply. You've shared my joys, my tears and my heart's inner musings. You are precious people whose wisdom I'll always seek. I love you.

● To my son Michael. My son, you've been an endless source of joy and fun in my life. Through the miracle of your birth and the wonder and amazement you've shown toward every new experience, you've taught me to appreciate all that's around me too. I love you.

● To my sisters and brothers, Melodie, Lynn, John and Philip. Thanks for your love and laughter, and your unselfish ways in my life. I think of each of you daily and remember the fullness of shared experiences.

● To my editor, Michael Warden, whose reviews of the manuscript offered much-needed positive criticism. You always brightened my day when you called. Thanks for the hard work, and for caring about and believing in me.

● To my friend, Ron Hawkins, who has faithfully supported, encouraged and prayed for my ministry and this project. You've been an oasis of inspiration for this project through your words, ideas and life.

● Finally, my deepest appreciation to the fine congregation at First Assembly of God in Fort Wayne, Indiana. My most grateful thanks for your prayers and support during this project.

CONTENTS

FAMILY DEVOTIONS; "OH, BOY!" or "OH, NO!"

Welcome to a new concept in family devotions! *Fun Devotions for Parents and Teenagers* was written for families who want family devotions without the boredom. These devotions aren't just to be read. Rather, they're to be experienced—by all the senses of each family member. Instead of an anecdote to start things off, how about a family game or a fun quiz? And rather than always just reading the Bible passage, make it fun by acting it out or drawing a picture to describe it. Then close the devotion by opening the family to new possibilities—family projects, fun ideas to do together, ways to drive the devotion's message home. Don't just talk about it. Do it!

Do the devotions in any order you want. Each devotion hits on a topic important to families. Choose the devotion each week that reflects your families present needs or concerns.

But I'm Not a Teacher!

Don't worry. These devotions have been carefully designed to involve all family members through "active" learning. That means the teacher becomes more of a guide and less of an instructor. The interaction in each activity promotes open communication and group-guided learning.

Consequently, these devotions take little or no preparation and involve only materials common to most households. The devotions are topical and focused. Each topic has been chosen because of its relevance to adults and teenagers. With these devotions, you'll cover a spectrum of issues— from AIDS to finances to servanthood. But all will provide fun and insightful family times.

But We've Never Done Devotions Before

You're not alone. But *Fun Devotions for Parents and Teenagers* makes it easy. The devotions are fun and involving. They cover topics that concern teenagers and parents alike. Here's one way to get your family started in using these devotions.

Explain the devotion process to family members. Then agree to a one-month trial run of weekly family devotions. When the month is over, get feedback from family members on how they feel about the content, time and location. Take their suggestions and commit to another month or more. It won't be long until the family looks forward to these intimate sharing times.

But We Don't Have Time

Twenty minutes. That's how long it takes to do most of these devotions. Some may take as long as 30 minutes, but others will take only 15. And you can control their length by adding or deleting discussion questions or activities as you see fit.

These devotions can be done daily or weekly, whatever suits your family best. You can even spread a single devotion over three days by doing one section of the devotion each day.

How to Use This Book

Before you launch into these devotions, there are a few things each family member should have: a Bible, a pencil, and a spiral notebook to use as a journal. Each family member needs to bring these items to every devotion.

The journal is a tool to help family members keep track of what they've studied. It's also a great way to keep thoughts and impressions all in one place. Directions for using the journal are given in individual devotions. But each one will follow a similar format. Before each devotion, have family members each write across the top of their journal page the devotion title and date. Then at the end of each devotion time, have family members reflect on the devotion by writing what they learned from the devotion and how they can apply it to their lives.

Each devotion is divided into seven sections to make it easy for the leader to use. Let's look at each of these sections:

Purpose: This section states the goal of the devotion.

Materials: Each person needs a Bible, journal, and pencil for every devotion. This section gives you a checklist of everything else you'll need.

Preparation: A few devotions require a little preparation before the devotion begins. In those cases, this section tells you exactly what you must do to prepare.

Get Ready: This section kicks off the devotion with a game, survey or other appropriate activity.

Get Set: This section incorporates a more serious activity and usually a family-study of Bible passages.

Go: This section gives suggestions for actions family members can take to apply the devotion to their lives. Prayer is always included here.

The Extra Mile: Each devotion concludes with ideas for further study or suggestions for even more ways to apply the devotion to family members' lives. These are often fun ideas to get the family to spend time together.

Creative Ideas for Using These Devotions

Use these tips for making your family devotions fun and meaningful for all:

Family night—Reserve a night each week for "family night." Begin with a game, such as volleyball, badminton or tennis, or play something indoors, such as a board game or cards. Then fix a meal together, or pack a picnic dinner and take off for the park. After relaxing together a while, launch into the devotion time.

Teenager-led devotions—Allow your teenager to lead devotions occasionally. Since the devotions are "active," the teenager won't need to lecture. But he or she will enjoy being in charge of the family time.

Family networking—Coordinate your use of this book with other families in your church or neighborhood. On health topics, such as AIDS, premarital sex or alcohol, join with these families and invite a guest speaker from your local Red Cross, police department or crisis pregnancy center.

Parent-teenager meetings—Youth workers can use this book for parent and teenager meetings. Embellish the devotions with games and activities to fill out the event.

What Now?

To make your family devotions the best times possible, follow these simple rules:

● Pray consistently for family members and your devotional time together.

● Avoid criticizing others' opinions or forcing your own opinions. Openness and security are important to the success of these devotions. The goal isn't necessarily to agree, but to discuss.

● Be enthusiastic! The attitude is contagious. It keeps away the deadly "This-is-stupids" and "I-don't-wannas."

● Don't fear silence or the tension that will inevitably arise from certain devotions. Silence offers people the chance to reflect on what someone has said or to reconsider their own positions on an issue.

● Enjoy yourself! If you have fun, it's more likely others will too. So savor this time together. Celebrate every laugh and every tear!

That's it! You've got all you need. Get ready, get set, go!

CAN WE TALK?

PURPOSE: To enhance family communication.

MATERIALS: You'll need 10 3×5 cards.

For each family member you'll need six 3×5 cards, a Bible, a pencil and a journal.

PREPARATION: Write each of the "Driving Tips" and "Communication Principles" on a separate 3×5 card to use in the Get Set section.

GET READY

Give family members each six 3×5 cards and a pencil. On three of their cards, have family members each put three different "who" questions, such as "Who likes anchovies?" or "Who shaves the hair on their kneecaps?" On the other three cards, have family members each write three different "why" questions, such as "Why do flying fish fly?" or "Why do we have eyebrows?" Have family members gather their cards face down in two stacks. Let one stack be the "who" questions and the other stack be the "why" questions. Redistribute the "who" cards, question side down. Instruct family members not to read the questions, but have them each write on the back of each card an answer to a "who" question. For example, they might write "President Washington" or "Toto."

Distribute the "why" cards and have family members follow the same procedure—only writing an answer to a "why" question on each card, such as "Because I said so" or "Because they mate in the spring."

When everyone is finished, have family members each

read the question and answer on each of their cards. Then ask:

● **When does poor communication really cause problems?**

● **What's the funniest situation you've ever experienced due to miscommunication?**

● **What two words best describe your communication style?**

Say: **Everyone wants to go places fast. Efficiency and speed are the premiums today.**

Lay out on the table the cards with the driving tips and communication principles.

Say: **Here are driving tips for getting around faster. Work together to match each driving skill with the corresponding communication skill.**

After family members have matched the cards correctly, say: **Read the cards again and put a plus sign (+) beside the communication principles you feel strongest in. Put a minus sign (−) beside the ones you need to work on.**

Write in your journal each skill you marked with a minus sign. Beside each one, list one thing you could do to improve in that area. For example, if you have trouble maintaining eye contact with others, you could try to determine the eye color of every person you talk to this week.

After everyone has finished writing, ask:

● **Why is it important for us to communicate effectively as a family?**

● **If you could change anything about the way we communicate, what would you change? Explain.**

Driving Tips	**Communication Principles**
1. Plan your travel route.	**A.** Proper Environment—A noisy, distracting place is not good for communication.
2. Pay attention to the signs.	**B.** Trustworthiness—Keep confidences. Show honest caring and concern. Avoid judgments and quick advice.
3. Avoid busy lanes.	**C.** Genuine Relationship—Consistent communication shows commitment and often requires forethought. Make communication a priority.
4. Avoid driving recklessly.	**D.** Mutual Respect—Understand teenagers' growing need for independence, but remember parents need to maintain their authority.
5. Respect the other driver.	**E.** Good Listening Skills—Maintain eye contact. Repeat what you thought was said. Note emotions and non-verbal communication. Be slow to speak—don't cut off or finish the other person's sentences.

(The answers: 1=C; 2=E; 3=A; 4=B; and 5=D.)

Have family members take turns reading aloud these scriptures: Romans 14:13, 19; Colossians 2:2-3; Ephesians 4:25-26; and 1 Corinthians 13:4-8a. Have family members discuss and record in their journals any insights about good communication.

Close the devotion by thanking God for each person's contribution to the family. Ask God to help each family member develop the skills necessary for good communication.

THE EXTRA MILE

Have weekly "Pow-Wows" with your family. Set aside a time and a place each week where family members sit in a circle and each share a "pow"—disappointment or frustration; and a "wow"—encouraging experience or fun event.

SPREAD THE WORD

PURPOSE: To learn practical ways to share Christ outside the home.

MATERIALS: You'll need a candle and matches.

For each family member you'll need paper, a journal, a pencil and a Bible.

PREPARATION: Plan to meet in a windowless room, or cover the windows to make the room dark.

GET READY

Gather the family around a table. Give each person a piece of paper and a pencil. Assign each family member one of the following "gospel story" scenes and have them each draw a sketch that represents their scene: Jesus' birth; Jesus' ministry (healing, teaching, performing miracles); Jesus' death; or Jesus' Resurrection.

When everyone is finished, have family members each describe their drawing and say one thing about that part of the gospel story they're thankful for.

After everyone has shared, have family members turn their papers over and divide them into four equal sections. Now have family members each draw their personal gospel story according to these four areas: when they met Jesus; what Jesus did for them; what Jesus does for them now; and what Jesus has done for them that they're most thankful for.

Have family members each share their gospel story and

explain each picture.

Ask:

● **How do you share Christ's love with others?**

● **Why is it sometimes hard to share Christ with others?**

Have family members each open their Bible on their lap. Light a candle and turn off the lights. Holding the candle, walk as far away from the family as possible and turn around so your back is toward them. Have family members try to read aloud from their Bibles. Now turn and walk slowly toward them. Have them each raise their hand when they can read their Bible.

Blow out your candle, turn on the lights and say: **Just as you couldn't read your Bible because you had no light, so non-Christians can't see Jesus unless we shine his light. Our good deeds and our testimony of what Christ has done in our lives provide the light people need to see Jesus.**

Read aloud Matthew 5:14-16. Ask:

● **In what ways has your "light" been hidden?**

● **What can you do to make your "light" shine brightly?**

Read aloud the following list of family projects and work with your family to choose at least one of them to start this week:

● Meet a neighbor. Go as a family with some fresh-baked cookies to a neighbor you don't know. Then look for later opportunities to speak with them. Perhaps invite them to your church.

● Help rebuild or repair an elderly or poor person's home.

● Take part in a church outreach program.

● Organize and direct a neighborhood clothing or food drive. Give the donations to a charitable organization.

● Sponsor a needy child through a Christian relief organization, such as Compassion International, 3955 Cragwood Dr., Box 7000, Colorado Springs, CO 80933—1-800-336-7676.

● Volunteer with the Salvation Army.

● Send cards, flowers, gifts and books to homebound people in your church.

● Plug into an AIDS hospice program in your area.

● Start a letter-writing ministry to people in prisons.

● Have "story hours" for your neighborhood children. Encourage other families to join you. Use clowning, pantomime, active songs, stories, and arts and crafts to communicate the gospel.

Close the devotion by passing around the lighted candle. Have whoever has the candle thank God for making each family member a light for Christ to others. Pray for boldness and creativity in finding ways to share Christ with those around you.

*T*HE EXTRA MILE

Work together as a family to memorize the "Roman Road to Salvation": Romans 3:23; Romans 6:23; Romans 5:8; Romans 10:9-10. Have family members quote the verses to each other and have them each incorporate the verses into their personal "story." Then have family members look for opportunities to share their faith.

I'M ANGRY!

PURPOSE: To discover proper ways to express anger in the family.

MATERIALS: You'll need two eggs, a saucepan and water.

For each family member you'll need a journal, a pencil and a Bible.

PREPARATION: None needed.

GET READY

Gather everyone together in the kitchen. Place an egg in a saucepan of water and put it on the stove to heat. Let the egg cook as you continue the devotion.

Have family members each number a page in their journal from one to eight. Say: **I'm going to read a series of statements. After each statement, write an "A" or a "D" beside the number that corresponds to the statement depending on whether you agree or disagree.**

Read aloud these statements, pausing between each one:

1. All anger is bad.
2. Good Christians shouldn't express anger.
3. It's childish to lose your temper.
4. There are good and bad ways to express anger.
5. When angry, you should try to forget about the situation and let time heal it.
6. No one can *make* me angry; I choose to respond to situations with anger.
7. Christians should express their anger differently than non-Christians.

8. I express anger incorrectly most of the time.
Ask:
  ● **Which statement was the most difficult to decide on?**
  ● **Which statement challenged you the most?**

Assign each family member one of the following passages. It's okay if more than one person is assigned the same passage. Have family members each write their scripture reference and the related question in their journal.
  ● *Ephesians 4:26-27*—What happens when you put off trying to correct a bad situation?
  ● *James 1:19-20*—How does being "slow to become angry" help bring about the righteous life God desires in you?
  ● *Matthew 5:21-24*—How does anger between people affect their relationship with God?
Have family members each read their passage, answer the question and list in their journal as many "anger busters"—ways to diffuse or control anger—as they can from their passage.
When everyone is finished, have family members each read aloud their passage, answer their question and share their anger busters. Have family members record all the anger busters in their journals.
Now take the egg out of the pan of boiling water and set it on the table. Also take a fresh egg from the refrigerator and set it on the table. Pick up the fresh egg and say: **I can enjoy this fresh egg in several ways. I can fry it, scramble it, boil it or use it with other ingredients to make a cake or a stack of waffles.**
Pick up the boiled egg and say: **This egg is not so versatile. In response to the heat, this egg has hardened. So now I can only use it in a few ways, such as in an egg salad or in deviled eggs.**

Ask:
* **When you respond incorrectly to angry feelings, what kind of "hardening" happens inside you?**
* **How does this hardening keep you from being all that God wants you to be?**

Read aloud the following situations. Then have family members discuss the questions.

Family Situation #1—Sally's mom rummaged through Sally's dresser looking for something. Sally is angry because she feels her mother invaded her privacy. She also remembers other times her mom looked through her drawers.
* **How should Sally respond to this situation?**

Family Situation #2—Dr. Roberts, a surgeon, just received an emergency call. As he gets in the car to leave for the hospital, he realizes the gas gauge is on empty. His son Tom used the car last night and came in past his curfew. Dr. Roberts has to stop for gas on the way to the hospital emergency.
* **How should Dr. Roberts deal with his anger and this situation?**

Family Situation #3—Sam just discovered his little brother wore Sam's favorite shirt and left a hole in it. His little brother often takes Sam's things without asking. As Sam heads for his brother's room, he thinks about how many times his brother has taken things. Sam gets angrier with each step.
* **How should Sam deal with his anger and this situation?**

After the discussion, close the devotion with prayer. Have family members pray to learn better ways to express their anger.

THE EXTRA MILE

As a family, draw up ground rules for expressing anger in your household. For example, some rules might be:

● All arguments must be resolved before you go to bed.
● Yelling is forbidden.

Make sure everyone knows the rules. Provide specific consequences for breaking any rule—such as suspended privileges or extra chores.

WITH ALL DUE RESPECT

PURPOSE: To understand the importance of respect among family members.

MATERIALS: You'll need an apple.

For each family member you'll need a Bible, a journal and a pencil.

PREPARATION: None needed.

GET READY

Have family members work together to create a human locomotive. Have each person become a different part of the locomotive, such as the furnace, the wheels, the smoke stack or even the door. Take a trip around the room or the house.

After the experience, ask:
- **What did you like about this experience?**
- **What did you dislike?**
- **What would've happened if everybody wanted to play the same role in our locomotive?**

GET SET

Say: **Let's talk about trains! A train needs several people to help it do its job: an engineer, a brake operator, a fuel manager, a conductor and a pas-**

senger. **I'll read a description of each of these jobs. Jot them down in your journal and decide which one most closely resembles the part you play in our household.**

● *The engineer*—This person manages the train, keeping it on time and directing its course. He or she coordinates the duties of everyone else on the train.

● *The brake operator*—This person is in charge of stopping the train and is constantly watching for any threats to the safety of others on the train.

● *The fuel manager*—This person is in charge of keeping the train fueled and moving at the speed dictated by the engineer.

● *The conductor*—This person communicates schedules and other important information to the passengers. He or she works to keep the passengers comfortable and happy.

● *The passenger*—This person rides the train and supports the railroad with finances. He or she enjoys the scenery and all the amenities the train has to offer.

Have family members each say what position they chose and why. Then have family members read the verses below that concern them.

Parents and teenagers: Proverbs 4:1; Proverbs 10:1; and Ephesians 6:1-4.

Husbands and wives: Proverbs 31:10-12, 25-31; 1 Corinthians 7:3-4; and Ephesians 5:21-28.

Ask:

● **What would happen if everyone wanted to be the "engineer" in our family? the "passenger"?**

● **How is this like life at home? How is it different?**

● **What would happen if we didn't respect each other's role in the family?**

Hold up an apple and say: **Take this apple and do something to it that demonstrates how you want oth-**

er family members to respect you. For example, you could polish the apple to demonstrate that you want others to encourage and recognize your good qualities.

After everyone has demonstrated his or her desire, ask each person:

● **How can you show respect to other family members?**

● **How will others' increased respect for you help you and encourage you?**

Pray that each family member would respect others in the family. Ask God to increase the love, trust and caring communication of family members. Praise God for his plan for the home and the strong relationships he can build there.

If your apple is still intact after the Go activity, share it as a symbol of togetherness and respect.

THE EXTRA MILE

Make apples your family's official "I respect you" gift! Have family members give apples to each other at special times, such as when someone needs an extra dose of encouragement or deserves special recognition for something he or she has done. For example, bake an apple pie for your teenager after a painful breakup with his or her steady. Or give your husband or wife an apple salad after the successful completion of a major project at work or home. Or leave an apple on a family member's pillow to remind that person you care.

TIME WITH GOD

PURPOSE: To encourage family members to spend time with God daily.

MATERIALS: For each family member you'll need a journal, a pencil and a Bible.

PREPARATION: None needed.

GET READY

Read aloud the following letter:

Dear Friend,

I'm writing to let you know I've missed you lately. I've called and called, and I've not been able to reach you. I've been in all the usual places we hung around together, but you don't seem to be in any of those places anymore. The last time you told me we'd get together, you never came!

I see the letters I sent you lying around unread. I just know if you started reading them, you'd be back speaking with me and hanging around with me because you'd know how much I care about you.

I see you struggling with so many things, and you're so confused it hurts me. I know I can help you, but you have to read my letters. You have to spend time with me or I can't help you.

I really hope you read this letter before we're so far apart you completely lose your desire to know me. I'll keep calling you. If you want to reach me, you know where I am—I haven't moved.

Sincerely,
Your Best Friend

After reading the letter, ask:

• **What were you feeling as I read this letter?**

• **How is ignoring a best friend like not spending time with God?**

• **In what ways does this letter apply to you?**

Have family members each draw in their journal, a scenic map describing their own spiritual journey so far. Have them start from the time they became Christians and continue through today. Display the "Spiritual Journey Example" on page 27 to give family members ideas. Tell them to note the years or months of "great beginnings," "spiritual mountaintops" and "lowlands."

After everyone is finished, have family members each explain their drawing. Then have family members each add a cross to their "spiritual journey" wherever their times of personal devotions were consistent. Ask:

• **How has your devotional time affected your spiritual journey?**

• **How would your spiritual journey change if you had consistent devotions all the time?**

Say: **Though there are many examples in scripture of the importance of a personal devotion time with God, Jesus' example is perhaps the strongest. Let's look at how Jesus felt about his personal devotional life.**

Have volunteers read aloud these scriptures: Matthew 14:22-24; Mark 1:35-37; Luke 6:12; and Luke 22:39-41. Then ask:

• **Why did Jesus pray for long periods of time—**

even through the night?

● **Do you think Christ's life was busy? Why or why not?**

● **How could a personal devotion time benefit you? List several ways in your journal.**

Have family members join hands in a circle, discuss family prayer needs and have a few minutes of silent prayer. Then have an assigned person close the prayer.

The Extra Mile

Set up a specific time each day—perhaps in the morning or before bedtime—for family members to each have their personal devotions. Start out with five minutes, then after a few weeks increase it to 15 minutes. Provide devotional helps and optional daily scripture readings for family members. Make personal devotions a part of your family's daily routine.

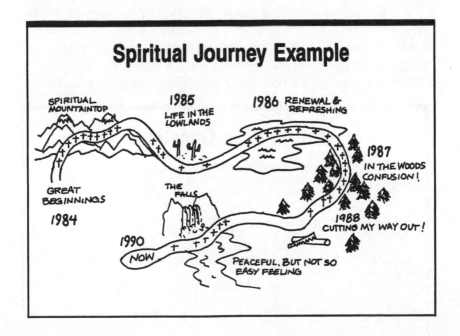

Spiritual Journey Example

SPIRITUAL MOUNTAINTOP

1985 LIFE IN THE LOWLANDS

1986 RENEWAL & REFRESHING

1987 IN THE WOODS CONFUSION!

GREAT BEGINNINGS 1984

THE FALLS

1988 CUTTING MY WAY OUT!

1990 NOW

PEACEFUL, BUT NOT SO EASY FEELING

TO TELL THE TRUTH

PURPOSE: To encourage family members to remain honest with each other.

MATERIALS: You'll need eight 3×5 cards and a marker. For each family member you'll need a journal, a pencil and a Bible.

PREPARATION: Number the 3×5 cards from one to eight.

GET READY

Gather everyone in a circle. Shuffle the numbered cards and stack them face down in the middle of the circle. Have family members each in turn draw the top card from the stack and read aloud the corresponding question from the "Truth or Lie Questions." Have them each decide whether

---

Truth or Lie Questions

1. Have you ever used an outhouse?
2. When being picked for a team sport, were you ever picked last?
3. Have you ever had your first, middle or last name mispronounced twice in the same day by someone?
4. Would you hang glide if you were given a chance?
5. Have you read at least four books of the Bible in the last year?
6. Have you ever loved two guys or girls at one time?
7. If you were 20 feet from shore would you dive into shark-infested waters for $1,000,000?
8. If you found a brown bag with $300 in it by the side of a country road, would you turn it in to the police?

they want to tell a lie or answer the question truthfully.
They then must answer yes or no, including a brief explanation of their answer—regardless of whether they told the
truth.

Have other family members write in their journals either "truth" or "lie" depending on how they feel the person
answered the question. Family members get 100 points for
each person they fool. Continue to draw cards until they're
gone. Recirculate cards if necessary to be sure everyone has
an equal number of chances.

After the game, ask:

● **Why is it so hard to be honest at times? What
makes it hard?**

● **Is there any such thing as a white lie? Explain.**

● **What would result from a society where everyone is usually deceptive and dishonest?**

GET SET

Give each person one of these scriptures: Colossians
3:9-10; 1 Corinthians 13:6; and Proverbs 12:22. Have family
members each read their scripture. Then have them each
create three columns on a page in their journal. In the left
column, have family members write the scripture reference.
In the center column have them write what the verse says
about dishonesty. In the far right column have them write
what the verse says about honesty.

After family members finish, have each create a stick-
person cartoon that illustrates their scripture. Have them
share their cartoons, then ask:

● **What happens when honesty in the family
breaks down?**

● **Why do you think God puts such a high premi-
um on honesty?**

Read aloud the following situations and have family members each write a response to each one in their journal.

Situation #1: You arrive home after curfew. You quietly check your parents' room and find them sleeping. The next morning your father asks you what time you got home. What's your response?

a. "Oh, it wasn't too late."

b. "I got in after curfew (truth), but it was because of car trouble (lie)."

c. Admit you came in after curfew and explain why.

Situation #2: Your daughter received a letter from a friend you feel has a bad influence on her. You were concerned when the letter arrived, so you steamed the letter open and read it. You did find some alarming information in the letter. Your daughter thinks one of her brothers steamed the letter open. How do you respond?

a. Don't say anything.

b. Admit you opened the letter, but explain your concern.

c. Admit you opened the letter and apologize.

Ask:

● **Is it ever appropriate to lie? Why or why not?**

● **Is it okay to lie to avoid punishment?**

● **What's the danger of using lies to deal with life's circumstances?**

● **Can a person lie and not have it affect other areas of life?**

Pray that each family member would strive to avoid using deception to handle life's circumstances.

THE EXTRA MILE

Have the family look at magazines or watch Saturday morning television together and pick out blatant dishonesty. Discuss differing ideas of honesty in our world.

SET THE DATE

PURPOSE: To contrast Christian and non-Christian dating.

MATERIALS: For each family member you'll need a Bible, a journal and a pencil.

PREPARATION: None needed.

GET READY

Have teenagers use the following questions to interview parents. If you have more than one teenager, have them take turns asking the questions.

For Married Parents	For Single Parents
1. What first interested you in Mom/Dad?	**1.** When you were a teenager, what was the first thing that interested you in someone?
2. What do you remember most about your first date together?	**2.** Describe your first date.
3. What did you enjoy doing the most while on dates?	**3.** What did you most enjoy doing on dates?
4. What was the most romantic thing Dad did for Mom when you were dating? Mom did for Dad?	**4.** What was the most romantic event of your teenage dating life?
5. Describe your funniest date.	**5.** Describe your funniest date.
6. What was the most embarrassing thing that happened to each of you while on a date?	**6.** What was the most embarrassing thing that happened to you while on a date?

 GET SET

Read aloud 1 Kings 11:1-4 and 2 Corinthians 6:14-16. Then say: **I'm going to read a series of statements. After each statement, indicate whether you agree or disagree with the statement by giving a "thumbs up" or "thumbs down."**

● Christian dating is really no different than non-Christian dating.

● Christian dating should involve serving and helping others—as well as enjoying yourselves.

● Under no circumstances should a Christian date a non-Christian.

● There are some places Christians shouldn't go on a date because of the unwholesome atmosphere.

● As long as a Christian couple avoids drugs and sexual activity, they can do anything a non-Christian couple does on a date.

● It's important to pray and read the Bible with those you date.

● It's important to set standards for dating before your first date.

Have family members discuss their answers, emphasizing points they disagree on. Ask:

● **Which ideas mentioned in the statements are new to you? What do you think of them?**

● **What's the purpose of dating? Explain.**

 GO

Have family members who date—or will be dating—make a list in their journals of "Unshakeable Unbreakables"—basic dating standards, such as "I will not stay out past 1 a.m." Also have those family members each make a list of "No Trespassing Zones"—places they will not go, to avoid temptation.

When finished, have family members each share their lists. Pray for those who're dating and for those who'll be dating soon. Pray they'll make wise dating decisions and follow God's leading in who they date.

*T*HE EXTRA MILE

Find activities that interest both your family members and your date, and arrange to do those things together as a group. For example, play tennis or putt-putt golf, or water ski together. Or go see a movie together. You could even have neighbors over and play volleyball or card games.

FOREVER LOVE

PURPOSE: To examine the nature of true love.

MATERIALS: For each family member you'll need a journal, a pencil, a red pen and a Bible.

PREPARATION: None needed.

GET READY

Say: **Love is greatly misunderstood in our society. Out of all the movies any of us have seen lately, let's choose three or four and examine how they define love.**

Once you've chosen the three or four movies, have family members think about the movies individually and find examples of these misconceptions about love: love is lust; love is sex; love is a feeling; love just happens; love is immediate; and love is temporary. Also have them find examples of proper perceptions about love: love is commitment; love is work; love is selfless; and love is beautiful. Then ask:

● **What are the most harmful aspects of the misconceptions we mentioned?**

● **How is true love different from the perceptions given in the movies? How is it similar?**

After family members have discussed the questions, say: **Find an object in the household that represents true love, such as a heart shape or wedding ring.**

When everyone returns, have family members each explain why their item represents true love. Ask:

● **Why are there so many different ideas of what**

true love is?

  ● **Is there one definition that encompasses them all? Explain.**

Have family members each draw 15 two-inch-wide hearts in their journal using a red pen. Have someone read aloud 1 Corinthians 13:4-7. As family members listen to the reading, have them each write a quality of true love in each of the hearts in their journal. After the reading, read the following list of 15 qualities of true love from the passage and have family members compare their responses.

Love is patient; is kind; isn't envious; isn't boastful; isn't proud; isn't rude; isn't self-seeking; isn't easily angered; keeps no record of wrongs; doesn't delight in evil; rejoices with the truth; always protects; always trusts; always hopes; and always perseveres.

Under each quality, have family members each write the name of a family member or friend who has most recently demonstrated that quality.

After everyone is finished, have family members share what they wrote and why.

Have family members each number in their journal from one to 11. Have a parent read aloud the following statements and have family members each respond to the statements by writing "yes" or "no" according to whether they think the statement describes true love.

  1. Love begins as a friendship, takes root and grows into something deeper.

  2. I accept the other person unconditionally.

  3. I trust him or her completely.

4. We enjoy being together around other people as well as being alone with each other.

5. I encourage my boyfriend or girlfriend or spouse to spend time with his or her friends and family.

6. We enjoy talking together.

7. We give each other private time and space—we don't feel we need to be with each other constantly.

8. We keep our talks confidential.

9. I want the best for the other person—even if I have to sacrifice.

10. The other areas of my life become more fruitful because of our relationship.

11. We enjoy doing things for each other without expecting anything in return.

Say: **Now look at your answers. If you have four or fewer "yes" answers, you show confusion about what true love is. Study 1 Corinthians 13 to get a handle on your perspective. If you have five to eight "yes" answers, you show a reasonably good understanding of what true love is. If you have nine to 11 "yes" answers, you have an excellent understanding of true love. Congratulations!**

Have family members each thank God for the qualities of true love they see in their relationships. Have them each pray for wisdom to discern true love and the power to give love to others.

THE EXTRA MILE

Have a family movie marathon! As a family, watch two or three movies that deal with love. After each movie, discuss the movie's portrayal of love and how the story line might've been different if "true" love had been portrayed accurately.

LOVE WAITS

PURPOSE: To discuss premarital sex.

MATERIALS: For each family member you'll need a journal, a pencil, a Bible and a 1-foot-square of aluminum foil.

PREPARATION: None needed.

GET READY

Read aloud the following list of reasons to wait for sex until marriage and have family members rate each reason from one to five in their journals (1=extremely good reason to wait; 5=no reason to wait at all).

- Your mom and dad tell you to wait.
- You might catch a sexually transmitted disease such as AIDS.
- You might get pregnant.
- You fear your parents' reaction.
- You're afraid of soiling your reputation.
- You want your husband or wife to be the first.
- You want to live by God's design.
- You don't want to damage your relationship with God.
- You fear God's judgment.
- You want to help develop patience in your life.
- You want to avoid guilty feelings.
- You want to feel good about yourself.
- You want to honor God with your body.
- You don't want a warped perception of what love is.
- You want to avoid comparing your future spouse to your past sex partners.

Now have family members go back and put stars by their top five reasons to wait for sex until marriage. Have family members each share their top five reasons. Ask:

● **With all these reasons to wait for sex until marriage, why do people have premarital sex?**

Give family members each a 1-foot-square of aluminum foil. Assign each of the following scriptures to family members: 1 Corinthians 6:18-20; Ephesians 5:1-3; and 1 Thessalonians 4:3-8. It's okay if more than one person has the same passage. Have family members each read their passage aloud and tell how the scripture applies to the issue of premarital sex. Then have family members each take their aluminum foil and shape it into a sculpture describing how the scripture passages make them feel. After everyone is finished, have family members each explain their sculpture.

Read aloud the following "sex lines." After reading each line, have family members come up with some "lines of resistance"—creative responses that might help people avoid being manipulated into having sex before marriage.

● If you loved me, you would.
● We both love each other, right?
● I love you enough to marry you.
● Everybody else is doing it.
● There are no virgins your age.

Close with prayer—asking God to help teenagers everywhere make wise choices about sex before marriage. Also pray that those who are already sexually involved will find God's forgiveness and begin making wise choices about sex.

THE EXTRA MILE

Speak to your youth minister about renting a teaching video on the dangers of premarital sex and showing it to your teenager's youth group. Offer to host the event in your home. Some examples of effective video resources for teenagers are "NO! The Positive Answer" (Word, Inc., Williams Square East Tower, 5221 N. O'Connor Blvd., Ste. 1000, Irving, TX 75039—214-556-1900) or "Wounded Lovers" (Video Research Institute, 550 High Street, Ste. 201, Auburn, CA 95603—1-800-223-4826). Preview any video you use with teenagers to prepare yourself for questions kids might ask.

FIGHTING AIDS

PURPOSE: To decide on a response to the AIDS crisis.

MATERIALS: For each family member you'll need a journal, a pencil and a Bible.

PREPARATION: None needed.

GET READY

Have family members draw a line down the middle of their journal page. On the left side have them write "Fair?" On the right side have them write "Still Fair?"

Say: **I'm going to describe a series of people who have AIDS. For each person, write "yes" or "no" under the "Fair?" column according to whether you feel it's fair for that person to have AIDS.**

Read aloud the list of people from the "Person With AIDS" column on page 41, pausing between each person. After everyone has responded, say: **Now I'm going to read a brief explanation of how each of these people got AIDS. After each explanation, write "yes" or "no" under the "Still Fair?" column according to how you feel after hearing the explanation.**

Read aloud the explanations under the "Explanation" column.

Ask:

● **Do you think you judged these people fairly? Why or why not?**

Read aloud Matthew 9:11-13 and John 8:3-11. Then ask:

● **How would Christ's perspective of these people differ from yours?**

Person With AIDS	Explanation
A prostitute	Had been sexually abused when young—ended up on the street
A baby	Parent had AIDS
A drug addict	Introduced to drugs when young by an older brother or sister
A friend	First-time sexual encounter he or she regretted anyway
A blood-bank worker	Came into contact with infected blood by accident
A homosexual	Sexually abused when young

Have family members each close their eyes and think about how it would feel to have AIDS. Read aloud the following paragraphs, pausing often to allow family members to reflect on what you're saying.

For a long time you've been feeling worn down and listless. You have a cold that won't go away. The strange sores on your body never heal. You had received a blood transfusion a few years ago, so during your regular physical you allowed the doctor to test you for AIDS. It's now several days later, and the doctor has asked you to come talk to her.

In the office, the doctor looks you right in the eyes and says, "There's no easy way for me to say this, but . . . you have AIDS."

It seems like a daze or a dream. Is this real? This couldn't happen to you, right? You hear broken fragments of what the doctor says—"Medical science can offer you some encouragement, but there's no cure yet."

Now it's over a year later and everyone who knows you knows that you have AIDS. Open your eyes and write in your journal your responses to these:

● When I ask myself, "Why me?" I feel . . .
● When no one visits me, I feel . . .
● When I see my body wasting away, I feel . . .
● When I think of how much life I haven't lived yet, I feel . . .
● When no one touches me, I feel . . .
● When someone says, "Just trust God," I feel . . .
● When I think of death, I feel . . .

Ask:
● **What were you feeling as we did this exercise?**
● **How has this exercise affected your thinking?**

Have someone read aloud Matthew 8:1-3. Ask:
● **How did Jesus react to the victim of leprosy—physically and verbally?**
● **What motivated his words and actions?**

Have someone read aloud Luke 7:36-48. Ask:
● **What can we learn from Jesus' response to this woman?**
● **What can we learn from these passages that we can apply to AIDS victims?**
● **How can our family get involved in caring for AIDS victims?**

After the discussion, close with a prayer for AIDS victims everywhere.

THE EXTRA MILE

Contact your local AIDS hospice program or AIDS support group. Find out how your family can get involved in helping AIDS victims in your area.

HYPOCRISY UNMASKED

PURPOSE: To help family members respond effectively to hypocrisy in themselves and others.

MATERIALS: You'll need a hand-held mirror.

For each family member you'll need a paper plate, a marker, a journal, a pencil and a Bible.

PREPARATION: None needed.

GET READY

Give family members each a paper plate and a marker. Have them each draw on their plate a face that shows the emotion *opposite* of how they feel. For example, a person who's feeling lighthearted would draw a sad face. Have family members punch holes in their masks for the eyes. Then have them each hold their mask over their face and keep it there. Have family members each explain the emotion portrayed on their mask. Then ask:

● **How often do you act like someone other than who you really are?**

● **What things do you do that aren't really "you"? Why do you do those things?**

● **What bugs you the most about hypocrisy?**

Read aloud the "Hypocrisy Opinionnaire" and have family members write their responses in their journals. Then discuss any differences of opinion and work to come to a consensus in that area. Then ask:

- **Why is it so hard to avoid hypocrisy?**
- **What can we do to fight hypocrisy in our lives?**

Hypocrisy Opinionnaire

1. Define "hypocrite."

2. Is it worse to be a hypocritical Christian or not to be a Christian at all? Explain.

3. Answer these "True" or "False":
- It's impossible for anyone to live the Christian life.
- If a person doesn't act like a Christian, he or she isn't one.
- All Christians have moments of hypocrisy.
- Hypocrites should be kicked out of the church.

Have volunteers read aloud these scriptures: Matthew 6:1-8; Matthew 7:1-5; and Luke 6:46-49. Then ask:

- **Why does God condemn living your life just to gain others' approval?**
- **What's wrong with measuring people by what we think they should be like?**
- **What's God's attitude toward judging others?**

Pass a hand-held mirror around the family. As family members each look into the mirror, have them say one way they'll allow others to see them without "masks." Ask God to show each of you where hypocrisy exists in your life. Thank the Lord that he can free people to be themselves.

THE EXTRA MILE

Take the family to a play. Watch how the actors pretend to be someone they're not. After the production, ask:
- **Can you tell what the actors are really like from the parts they played? Why or why not?**
- **How does that relate to us wearing masks in everyday life?**
- **Why is it so easy to hide behind masks?**

GOD'S PRIZE

PURPOSE: To see our lives from God's perspective.

MATERIALS: You'll need aluminum foil and paper.

For each family member you'll need a journal, pencil and Bible.

PREPARATION: None needed.

GET READY

Give each family member four or five single square-foot sheets of aluminum foil. Starting with the tallest person and going clockwise, have the first person make a "happy face" and then shape the foil around his or her expression to make a foil sculpture. After family members each have done a happy face, have them try other "faces," such as a "surprise face," a "sad face," an "ugly face" or an "angry face." At the end, let family members vote on who shaped the best face. Award that person a wad of foil made from all the other sculptures. Ask:

● **How is this exercise like the way others sometimes perceive you?**

● **How do others' perceptions of you affect your behavior?**

GET SET

Give each person a piece of paper and have them each form a sculpture that represents how God sees them. They can tear, fold and otherwise shape it. When everyone is finished, read aloud 1 Samuel 16:7. Ask:

● **How did you feel when you viewed yourself from God's perspective?**

● **Why is it so hard to accept ourselves the way God does?**

● **What can we do to change wrong thinking about ourselves?**

Read aloud Psalm 139:1-16, pausing briefly between each verse. Then ask each person:

● **What does this passage say to you about God's design for you and your life?**

Say: **Imagine God has decided to write you a letter about what a unique creation you are and his desire to have a relationship with you. Write what you think God would say. Read Psalm 139:1-16 to get started.**

After everyone is finished, form a circle. Have family members each tear a blank page from their journal and write their name at the top. Have them divide the page into four equal sections. In each section, have them write one of these open-ended statements:

● The qualities you bring to our family no one else does are . . .

● The things you do best are . . .

● The qualities you have to offer the world are . . .

● The thing I appreciate most about you is . . .

Then have family members each pass their sheet to the family member on their right, and have them each write a brief response to each statement. Continue around the circle until each person has written on all the other family members' sheets.

Pray that family members would realize their value in God's eyes and would accept their uniqueness in him.

Thank God for the rich blessings he has given your family in each individual.

THE EXTRA MILE

Have a "We Celebrate You" day! Set aside a day each month for one family member to be "celebrated." On that day have another family member take over that person's chores. Fix the celebrated person's favorite meal. Allow him or her to control the TV programming for that evening. Give the person a card telling how special and loved he or she is.

PRAYER TEAM

PURPOSE: To encourage family members to pray for each other.

MATERIALS: You'll need a legal pad.

For each family member you'll need a journal, a pencil and a Bible.

PREPARATION: None needed.

GET READY

Have family members each number from one to six in their journals. Then read aloud the following survey and have family members write a response to each item.

1. What one word best describes your prayer life?

2. Christians should spend _____ minutes in prayer per day.

3. I _____ (often, sometimes, never) pray.

4. It's _____ (easy, hard) for me to pray.

5. I believe God _____ (always, sometimes, never) answers my prayers.

6. When I pray, I usually pray for_____.

After the survey, have family members share their answers. Ask:

- **What's your biggest struggle in prayer?**

GET SET

Have volunteers read aloud these scriptures: 2 Corinthians 1:8-11; James 5:16; and 2 Thessalonians 1:11-12. Have family members each create two columns in their journal and list the scripture references in the left column. In the right column have them each list the benefits of praying for others based on the verses. Ask:

● **How do you feel when you know others are praying for you?**

● **How will praying for others help you understand them better?**

● **How can praying for each other promote love and unselfishness in our family?**

Draw a chart on the legal pad like the example on page 51. Hang the legal pad inside a cupboard door in the kitchen.

Tell family members they can write on the chart any requests they'd like the family to pray about. Decide on a specific time each week when family members will gather to pray for the requests on the chart and any other requests that may come up.

Ask family members each to share a prayer request. As they do, write their request on the prayer chart. Then pray together for the requests and for God to help family members pray together faithfully.

THE EXTRA MILE

Create personal prayer request diaries in basic spiral notebooks. Have family members each create three columns: Date, Request, Answer. Encourage family members to faithfully record their prayer requests and answers in their prayer journals. It's a great faith strengthener!

Prayer Chart

Date	Person	Request

FAMILY FORGIVENESS

PURPOSE: To show the importance of forgiveness within the Christian family.

MATERIALS: You'll need six 3×5 cards, an 8½×11 piece of corrugated cardboard and scissors.

For each family member you'll need a Bible, a 3×5 card, a journal, a pencil and a push pin.

PREPARATION: Write each of the "Would You Forgive Them?" situations on a separate 3×5 card to use in the Get Ready section. Use the scissors to cut a cross shape out of the cardboard.

GET READY

Spread the "Would You Forgive Them?" cards on the table so everyone can see them. One by one, have each person pick the three cards that describe situations in which they'd most likely forgive someone. Have them explain their reasons and return the cards to the table for the next person.

After each person has shared, repeat the process, except have each person choose the three situations they'd have the hardest time forgiving. Ask:

● **Why is it easier to forgive some sins than others?**

● **Do you think the distinctions we make between sins are appropriate? Why or why not?**

Would You Forgive Them?

- Mrs. Jones steals food for her hungry family.
- Fifteen-year-old Rita shoplifts with a group of friends for kicks.
- Judy takes home supplies from work for her personal use.
- Mary steals money from a wealthy home where she's babysitting.
- Mike steals to support his drug habit.
- Perry steals your time. He promises to meet you for lunch but doesn't show up.

Assign one of the following scriptures to each family member: Psalm 103:8-13; Matthew 18:21-22; Mark 11:25; and Ephesians 4:32.

Have each person read the scripture aloud, give a modern example that illustrates the passage, and tell what the passage means to him or her.

When everyone has shared, ask:

● **Why is it important to be forgiven when you hurt others?**

● **What would happen if family members refused to forgive each other?**

● **What difference does knowing God forgives your sins make?**

Read aloud Psalm 139:23-24. Give family members each a 3×5 card. Have them each write a sin for which they need God's forgiveness, then fold the card and tack it to the cardboard cross. Ask:

● **How did this exercise resemble Christ's sacrifice on the cross?**

● **How do you feel knowing God has forgiven you for the sin you just confessed?**

Close by praying for one another. Thank God for the forgiveness Christ provides and for the blessings he brings to forgiving families.

Don't look at the cards after the devotion. Burn them or tear them into small, unreadable pieces. Completely destroying them is another symbol of God's forgiveness.

THE EXTRA MILE

Have family members each write in their journals things they have trouble forgiving other people for. Have them ask God to give them a forgiving spirit, and encourage them to express their forgiveness to at least one person when they're ready.

THE LIGHT OF EASTER

PURPOSE: To experience the new life of the Resurrection.

MATERIALS: You'll need a dark closet or room, a large candle and matches.

For each family member you'll need a small candle, a Bible, a journal and a pencil.

PREPARATION: Become familiar with the Get Ready section so you can lead it in the dark.

GET READY

Gather the whole family in a small, dark room or closet. Sit in silence for several minutes. Then say: **Imagine what it would be like to live in darkness like this all the time.**

Ask:

● **What feelings do you have when you're in darkness?**

● **How is darkness like death?**

● **If your world was always dark, how much would light be worth to you?**

Open the door quickly. When you've adjusted to the light, leave the closet and read aloud John 19:38—20:20. Ask:

● **What feelings do you think the disciples had while Jesus was in the tomb? How were those feelings similar to or different from your feelings in the dark?**

● **What feelings did you have coming into the light that the disciples might have experienced after the Resurrection?**

Give everyone five minutes to search for items that represent new life, such as a flower or a picture of a baby. Gather everyone together and ask people each to share their items, explaining why they picked them. Ask:

● **How do these symbols resemble the miracle of the Resurrection?**

Have a family member read Romans 6:3-4. Ask:

● **What encouragement do you gain from Jesus' Resurrection?**

● **How does it feel to know the same power that raised Jesus from the dead has raised you to new life?**

● **What qualities of this new life do you see in yourself and those around you?**

Give each person a small candle, and set a large candle in the middle of a table. If possible, dim or turn off the lights. Say: **As I light your candle, share one reason you're grateful for the Resurrection and one reason you're grateful to be in our family.**

In turn, light family members' candles, beginning with the youngest and working to the oldest.

Continue until everyone has shared. Then have everyone simultaneously light the big candle to symbolize unity in Christ because of the Resurrection. As a family, sing the chorus "Alleluia" or another familiar praise song.

Say a prayer of thanksgiving for the unity, love and abundant life that came to your family as a result of the Resurrection.

THE EXTRA MILE

Have your family—or join with another family if you don't have enough people—create a short Easter drama based on John 19:38—20:20 and Romans 6:3-4. Then do it in a program for the children of your church, at a local children's hospital or nursing home, or even for a shut-in. Be sure to call the nursing home or shut-in in advance.

GROWING THROUGH FAILURE

PURPOSE: To remind family members that God loves them even when they fail.

MATERIALS: You'll need four 3×5 cards, a deck of cards, a 100-piece puzzle, a clock with a second hand or stopwatch, and a set of clothes—shoes and all—from the largest family member.

For each family member, you'll need a Bible, a journal and a pencil.

PREPARATION: Write the project descriptions from the Get Ready section on individual 3×5 cards. Lay the supplies for the Get Ready section on the floor beside the table.

GET READY

Put the 3×5 cards with the following project descriptions face down on the table:
- Make a 12-inch-tall house of cards.
- Assemble the puzzle.
- Completely change into another family member's clothes.
- Count how many times the word "the" appears in Genesis 1—3.

Have each family member select one card. If you have more than four people, form pairs to work on some projects.

Give family members only 40 seconds to complete their projects. Then gather together and ask:

● **What thoughts went through your head when you realized you'd fail to finish the project in time?**

● **When have you recently experienced similar feelings of failure?**

● **How do you respond when you fail?**

● **How do high expectations make it easier to fail?**

Say: **The Bible is filled with stories of people who failed. And it tells how God responds with compassion.** Assign different family members the following passages: Luke 22:31-34; Luke 22:54-62; and John 21:15-17.

After each passage is read aloud, have all family members indicate how close or far Peter felt from God during that time using the following:

● hands far apart to show Peter feeling completely separated from God; or

● hands clasped together to show Peter feeling intimate with God.

Discuss why each person chose a certain distance. Ask how Peter might have felt in each situation—and how Jesus might have felt. Then ask:

● **What can we learn about responding to other people's failures from Jesus' response to Peter?**

● **How does Peter's story encourage you in your struggle to deal with failures in your life?**

● **What can our family learn from Peter's story to support each other?**

Have family members each write a haiku in their journals about coping with failure. A haiku is a three-line poem

with: five syllables in the first line; seven syllables in the second line; and five syllables in the third line.

Here's an example to read to the family:

Failure does plant seeds,
Seeds of despair or success,
Choose which ones will grow.

Ask family members to share their haikus. Then ask:

● **Why did you focus your haiku the way you did?**

● **What other thoughts about failure did you leave out of your haiku?**

● **How can you learn to cope better with failures when they happen?**

Close with prayer, asking God to give each family member the grace to let others fail and to encourage them to grow through failure.

THE EXTRA MILE

Have family members clip stories from the newspaper about people who've failed themselves, others or God in some way. Also have family members list ways they let others down.

At the end of the week, pray together that each family member and the people in the news will receive God's grace so they'll have the strength and courage to learn from their failures.

IS ABORTION EVER RIGHT?

PURPOSE: To discuss perspectives on abortion and how to respond as a Christian.

MATERIALS: You'll need a bowl.

For each family member you'll need an egg, a Bible, a fine-point marker, a journal and a pencil.

PREPARATION: None needed.

GET READY

Gather everyone around a table. Divide the table into four sections and designate the sections: strongly agree, agree, disagree and strongly disagree.

Read aloud the statements in "The Abortion Debate" box, and have family members each respond by placing a

---

The Abortion Debate

1. Abortion is murder.

2. The choice to have an abortion is a personal matter for a pregnant woman.

3. A pill that induces abortion should be available to anyone.

4. Abortion is okay if you're raped or your life is in danger.

5. Abortion isn't okay for me, but it might be okay for someone else.

6. Abortion is an appropriate birth-control method.

7. If a baby will be deformed or retarded, abortion may be the best option.

hand in the appropriate table section. Give people a chance to explain their choices.

Discuss differences in responses. Then ask:
- **Which statements disturb you? Explain.**
- **Which statements were most difficult to respond to? least difficult? Why?**
- **What other factors—if any—might change your answers?**

Give family members each an egg and a fine-point marker. Assign each person one of the following scriptures. If you have passages left over, give some people two. Form pairs if you have more people than the following passages: Genesis 1:27; Deuteronomy 19:10; Psalm 127:3-5; and Psalm 139:13-16.

Have people each read their passage and write on their egg what the passage says about God's view of life. Have people each read their scripture aloud and share insights they gained.

When everyone has shared, have them throw their eggs into a bowl to break the eggs. Ask:
- **How is this illustration similar to and different from abortion? Explain your answer.**
- **Is it ever appropriate to take another person's life? Why or why not? If so, when?**

Have a family member read the case studies in the "What Should She Do?" box. After each one, decide as a family what the person should do and why. Be sure to think through the implications of each choice.

Close with prayer. Thank God for the precious gift of

What Should She Do?

Case Study #1—A 40-year-old woman discovers she's pregnant. Her last pregnancy—10 years ago—had problems, and her doctor warns of possible life-threatening complications this time. What should she do? Why?

Case Study #2—A 21-year-old single mother on welfare has four children and is pregnant again. She just completed training for a job that could get her out of her drug-infested housing project. But she won't be able to work if she has a baby. What should she do? Why?

Case Study #3—A 12-year-old girl becomes pregnant by a relative who sexually abuses her. What should she do? Why?

Case Study #4—A 17-year-old Christian girl gets pregnant when she and her boyfriend ''accidently'' have sex. She wants to get an abortion so ''one little mistake'' won't ruin her future plans and humiliate her family. What should she do? Why?

life. Pray for compassion for each family member to help those with unwanted pregnancies. And pray for wisdom in responding to today's difficult issues from a Christian perspective.

THE EXTRA MILE

As a family, talk with a doctor—either one who does or does not perform abortions, or both—about the abortion issue. Listen sensitively to his or her perspective. You might also want to talk with a counselor from a rape crisis center, a social worker, an adoption counselor, a minister or someone from a crisis pregnancy center.

OH, BROTHER! OH, SISTER!

PURPOSE: To encourage harmonious relations between brothers and sisters.

MATERIALS: For each family member you'll need a 3×5 card, a Bible, a journal and a pencil.

PREPARATION: On separate 3×5 cards, write the titles of children's songs everyone in your family knows, such as "Row, Row, Row Your Boat," "Mary Had a Little Lamb," or "Three Blind Mice." Make one card with a different children's song title for each family member.

GET READY

Give each family member a card with a different children's song title. Have all family members try to sing their songs at once. After several noisy attempts, ask:

● **Was it easy to keep singing your song when others were singing something different? Explain.**

● **Did you sing louder so everyone could hear you? Why?**

Say: **It's hard to be "harmonious" when everyone's competing and singing different tunes. The way we get along better is to harmonize and work together.**

Then lead a couple of rounds of "Row, Row, Row Your Boat" to illustrate your point.

GET SET

Assign family members one of the following scripture passages: Genesis 4:1-12 (Cain and Abel); Genesis 25:21-34 (Jacob and Esau); and Genesis 37:2-36 (Joseph and his brothers).

Have family members each read their passage and write a half-page diary entry in their journal as though they were a character in the story. When people are finished, have them read their passages and share what they wrote. Ask:

● **When have you felt like one of these characters? Which one? Why?**

● **How are the sibling rivalries in these passages similar to rivalries you've experienced? different?**

● **How could people in these stories resolve their rivalries?**

● **When have you been most angry with or jealous of a brother or sister? How did you deal with the situation?**

GO

Read Ephesians 4:25-27 aloud. Ask:

● **What important advice does this passage provide to feuding brothers and sisters?**

Tell family members to draw two columns on a page in their journals. As a family, brainstorm areas where sibling rivalries sometimes occur in your family, such as bathroom use or competition in school. List them in the left column.

When you've developed a list of eight to 10, brainstorm ways to resolve the rivalries harmoniously and fairly, such as set a time limit on bathroom use or encourage each other to do great in school. List the ideas in the right column.

After you've finished the two lists, work together to write a song that affirms each person's place in your family.

Sing it to the tune of "The Alphabet Song" or "Row, Row, Row Your Boat."

Close with prayer, asking God to unify your family and heal any anger, resentment or competition that exists.

THE EXTRA MILE

Through the coming week, have each family member give secret presents to all other family members. You don't need to give things that cost money. Someone can make a brother's bed, fix breakfast for a sister, do laundry for a parent or cook a special treat for a child.

FAMILY FIGHTS

PURPOSE: To learn creative ways to resolve family conflicts.

MATERIALS: You'll need a marker, masking tape, one die and six empty cans or jars.

For each family member you'll need paper, a Bible, a journal, a pencil and six paper strips (about 1×4 inches).

PREPARATION: Label the cans or jars #1 through #6 using a marker and masking tape.

GET READY

Have each family member tear a piece of paper into a shape that symbolizes the last time your family argued or fought. The design could represent emotions, what happened during the disagreement or the issue being discussed. For example, if the fight was over curfews, someone could tear the paper into a round shape to represent a clock.

Ask a family member to read aloud Romans 12:2, 10, 18. Ask:

• **What's the main thought of each verse?**

• **Why are these thoughts important to remember when people discuss tough topics?**

• **Why is it important to talk about some things even though they may be unpleasant?**

GET SET

Give each family member a pencil and six paper strips. Read aloud the following categories of "hot topics": (1) clothing and appearance; (2) dating and friendships; (3) home responsibilities; (4) entertainment; (5) privacy and personal rights; and (6) discipline. Have each person think of one conflict you've had in your family in each area. For example, for entertainment someone might write, "We always watch Monday night football, so I can't watch my favorite sitcom." As people finish, have them put their strips in the appropriate can or jar by number.

Say: **We're each going to roll a die. Whatever number you choose, draw a paper strip from the can with that number. Read the statement and try to think of a creative way to resolve the conflict. If you roll the number of an empty can, roll again.**

Start with the person with the cleanest shoes, and continue until you've dealt with all the situations. If someone has trouble thinking of a solution, have other family members brainstorm ideas too. Throughout the discussion, keep focused on the problem instead of attacking each other.

Afterward, ask:

● **Was it easy or difficult to discuss conflict? Explain.**

● **How did you feel as you discussed these issues?**

● **What did you learn about yourself and our family from this exercise?**

GO

As a family, brainstorm guidelines for how you treat each other when you disagree and how you resolve conflict. Some ideas you might list include:

● Always listen carefully before responding.

- Respect each other's opinions even when you disagree.
- Never physically hurt another person.
- Try to meet everyone's needs through compromise.

Have people list the guidelines in their journals. You may even have an artistic family member make a wall hanging or poster of the guidelines to hang in your kitchen as a reminder.

Close with a circle prayer in which family members each pray for the person on their right. Also pray that God will teach family members to be tolerant of differences and supportive of diverse opinions in the family. Ask God to unite and solidify your family through open discussion of conflicts.

THE EXTRA MILE

Have checkpoints through the week to see how well you've been able to follow the guidelines you've established. Celebrate any successes or changes you've noticed. Talk about ways to solve new problems.

TALENT SEARCH

PURPOSE: To learn about each other's talents and interests.

MATERIALS: You'll need a watering can with water.

For each family member, you'll need a facial tissue, a drinking straw, a paper plate, a spoon, a cotton ball, a Bible, a journal, some seeds (bean, pea or radish), a paper cup and some potting soil.

PREPARATION: None needed.

GET READY

Announce that this devotion begins with events from the Oh-Laughing Games. Have each person "compete" in the following events:

● Shot put—Using proper shot-put form, see how far you can hurl a balled-up facial tissue.

● Javelin toss—Launch a drinking straw across the room.

● Discus throw—Hurl a paper plate as though it were a discus.

● Pole vault—Use a spoon to catapult a cotton ball as far as possible. (Anyone who's ever been in a food fight knows how to do it.)

Ask:

● **What new "talent" did you discover in the games? Which event would you say was your best?**

● **What unknown talents did you see in other family members?**

Have someone read aloud Psalm 139:13-16 and Matthew 25:14-30. Discuss how God has created each person to be unique.

Have family members each make four columns on a page of their journal and label their columns as follows:

Three things I'm good at:	Three things I'm interested in:	Three activities I enjoy:	A dream I have for the future:

Have people each write in each column their responses to the statement. Then have them each pass their journal around so other people can add positive ideas to the first two columns. Then ask:

● **What did you learn about yourself from other people?**

● **What gives you the most fulfillment in life?**

Give family members each a seed and a paper cup filled with potting soil. Have them each write their name on their cup. Say: **The talents God has given us are like seeds. We must plant them in the rich soil of God's kingdom. We have to take care of them. And we must ask God to shower them with nourishment.**

Ask people each to choose one seed of a talent they want to grow to bear fruit for God's kingdom. Focus on one person at a time, by having each person answer these three questions:

- **What talent do you want to grow in your life?**
- **How can you nurture it in God's kingdom?**
- **What are some ways you can take care of it?**

Then have him or her plant the seed. As a family, pray that person's talent will grow with God's blessing. After the prayer, water the seed to symbolize God's work in the person's life.

Continue until each person has planted his or her seed.

THE EXTRA MILE

Keep the seeds in a well-lit window. As they grow, talk about the talents they represent and how people each are nourishing their talent. Celebrate accomplishments related to family members' talents.

FUN FAMILY MEMORIES

PURPOSE: To share family memories.

MATERIALS: You'll need one die.

For each family member you'll need eight photographs, a Bible, a journal and a pencil.

PREPARATION: For each person in your family, gather eight photographs from your family photo album.

GET READY

Have the family sit in a circle. Put the photographs face down in the center of the circle. Have family members each pick eight photographs, then have them each use their pictures to tell a madeup story. All the people in all the photos must be used. Encourage family members to be as creative as possible.

GET SET

Play the Wheel of Memories Game. Have each family member find a small item in the house to use as a playing piece. Open this book to the game board (page 74) and set it in the center of the circle. Set weights on the edges of the book to hold it open. Have family members take turns rolling the die to determine how many spaces to move. Players can move in any direction but must follow the instructions

Wheel of Memories Game

What's the craziest thing you've ever done?

Share your favorite memory of dating.

Tell about a time you were really bored.

What's the meanest thing you've ever done?

Share your saddest memory.

What's one thing you enjoy doing with the family?

What's your favorite memory of your father?

What's the dumbest thing that's ever happened to you?

Start

Share your favorite memory.

Tell about the time you've been most afraid.

What was the hardest time in your life?

Tell about a time you were proud of yourself—and why.

What's your favorite memory of your mother?

What one thing about your past would you change if you could?

Share your most embarrassing moment.

Tell about your favorite time with a sibling.

on the space where they land. All answers must be true. If a question really doesn't apply, roll again.

The game isn't competitive and has no finish line, so set a time limit. Start with the person with the longest hair.

After the game, ask each person:

- **How did it feel to share your memories?**
- **What memory did you most enjoy sharing? Why?**
- **What memory was hardest to share? Why?**
- **How does it help the family to share memories?**

Have different family members read aloud these passages: Philippians 1:3; and 4:8; and 1 Thessalonians 1:2-3. Ask:

- **How do these verses apply to a person's view of the past?**

After everyone has responded, have family members each share one memory of a time another family member did something special for them or taught them a valuable lesson.

Close by having family members each say a one-sentence "thank you" prayer for each family member.

THE EXTRA MILE

Try these ideas for family fun:

- Find a place your family has fond memories of and hold the devotion there. It may be a special room in the house or a nearby vacation spot.
- Take the family on a drive around town, remembering things you've done together at various locations.

FAMILY PRIORITIES

PURPOSE: To examine family priorities and the foundation they provide for the family.

MATERIALS: You'll need old magazines to cut up, a large piece of paper, glue, 10 pebbles, scissors, a marker, and a small container of sand.

For each family member, you'll need a journal, a Bible and a pencil.

PREPARATION: None needed.

GET READY

Say: **We're going to have an auction today. Each person has $168 to spend. Each dollar represents one hour during the coming week. Decide how much you'd spend on each item and bid on those things that are important to you. Remember, you can only spend $168.**

Read the list from the "Going Once, Going Twice" box, and have people think about what they want to bid on. Then auction off the items. If you wish, substitute or add other items that fit your family better. Keep track of how much people spend and what they buy. Continue until people have spent all their money or until all objects are gone. Afterward, ask:

● **Did you buy the things you really wanted? Why or why not?**

● **Did you buy some things you don't spend time**

on most weeks? Why or why not?

● **What did the auction show you about your personal priorities?**

● **How are the choices we make in our family similar to and different from the choices in the auction? Explain.**

Going Once, Going Twice

Working	Watching television	Sleeping
Eating	Playing	Studying
Exercising	Talking together	Reading
Doing chores	Going to church	Spending time with God
Visiting with friends	Shopping	Doing hobbies

GET SET

Say: **In the same way individuals have priorities, so do families. We make choices together about what's important to us and what we'll do.**

Brainstorm your family's top 10 priorities. Try to come to a consensus on the order. Then have family members go through old magazines together and select pictures that represent those choices. Use large paper, glue and scissors to make a collage of the pictures. Title the creation, "What's Important to Us."

Have someone read aloud Matthew 7:24-27. Place your priority collage on the table. As a family, decide whether each priority is a "rock" priority or a "sand" priority. If it's a rock priority, put a pebble on top of the picture. If it's a sand priority, put sand on top of it. Ask:

● **In general, do our priorities provide a firm or a weak foundation for our family? Explain and give examples.**

● **How might our family be able to shift from pri-**

orities that form a weak foundation to priorities that form a strong foundation?

Have family members each write your family's top 10 priorities in their journal, leaving space to write between each one. Then ask people each to write two ways they personally can help accomplish each priority. When everyone is finished, have people read what they can do in each area.

Close by praying that God will help each family member discover the joy of building your home on the rock of Jesus Christ.

THE EXTRA MILE

Have family members each keep track of their time during the coming week. Then discuss how all of you spent your time, what priorities you followed and how you might alter your time commitments to fit your priorities more completely.

WHERE ARE WE GOING?

PURPOSE: To learn the importance of working together toward family goals.

MATERIALS: You'll need two blindfolds for every three people, six pieces of paper and markers.

For each family member you'll need 12 3×5 cards, a Bible, a journal, a pencil and a tool.

PREPARATION: None needed.

GET READY

Say: **We have several chores to do before the devotion. But instead of assigning jobs, everyone will help on the same task.**

Assign each person one of the following roles (more than one person can have each role):

● Talker—can only talk; wears a blindfold and can't do anything.

● Doer—can only do things; wears a blindfold and can't talk.

● Seer—can see, but can't do anything except whisper to the Talker.

Get people ready for their roles. Blindfold everyone but the Seers. Then have everyone do two or three chores around the house together. For example, family members could sweep the kitchen floor, make a bed or dust the living room furniture. Then ask:

● **What was most fun about this experience? least fun?**

● **What did you learn about working together on a common task?**

● **How is this experience similar to working together in the family? different?**

Give each person 12 3×5 cards and a pencil. Place six pieces of paper on a table. Title them "Spiritual," "Relational," "Social," "Physical," "Financial" and "Intellectual."

On their cards, have people each describe your family in each of the areas on the papers (one card per area). For example, for "Spiritual," someone might write, "We attend church regularly and have weekly family devotions." Have people put their cards face down on the appropriate piece of paper on the table. When everyone's finished, read and discuss each stack.

Then have people each write on new cards one thing the family needs in each area. To do this, have people ask themselves, "What would I change about our family if I could?" Read and discuss responses.

Based on the needs mentioned, brainstorm together what goals you'd like to have for your family. Write all the ideas on the paper for that category. Then choose the top three priorities in each category, and put stars beside them. Write dates for accomplishing these goals. Ask:

● **What do the goals we've chosen say about our family?**

● **How will these goals affect you personally?**

● **How can you help our family meet its goals?**

Read aloud Nehemiah 2:11-20. Say: **Nehemiah returned to Jerusalem after it had been destroyed. He set goals**

for rebuilding the city with God's help. Our family isn't in ruins like Jerusalem, but we too can build our family with God's help.

Give each person a tool. Ask:

● **What will you give to help build our family toward its goals?**

As family members each respond, have them place their tool in the center of the table.

Hold hands and pray together, asking God to give each family member the strength and vision to work together for the goal of building up the family.

THE EXTRA MILE

Type your family goals and put them in a high-traffic area of your home. Review the list regularly, and talk about how your family has improved because of the goals you set. Then go out and celebrate!

DO YOU HEAR WHAT I HEAR?

PURPOSE: To help family members develop their listening skills.

MATERIALS: For each family member you'll need a journal, a pencil and a Bible.

PREPARATION: If you can, have this devotion outside where you'll hear a greater variety of sounds.

GET READY

Say: **It's sure noisy around here. Oh, it might not seem noisy, but this room is filled with noises. Listen to all the sounds you hear in the next five minutes. Whenever you hear a sound, write it in your journal. If you hear a sound you don't recognize, just describe it.**

Sit in silence for about five minutes. Then have family members report what they heard. Ask:

● **Did any of the sounds you heard surprise you? Explain.**

● **Why did you hear sounds just now you're around all the time but don't usually hear?**

● **What did this experience tell you about the way we interact in the family?**

● **When was the last time you felt really listened to? How did you know the person was listening closely? How did you feel?**

GET SET

Assign each family member a different listening skill from the "Five Keys to Great Listening" box. It's okay if family members have more than one skill or if some have no skill assigned to them. Don't show family members the other listening skills, and tell them to keep their skill secret.

Have family members find one partner for each skill they have. For example, if a family member has two listening skills, he or she would find a partner for the first skill and a separate partner for the second skill. Have partners each decide how to form a human statue to illustrate their listening skill.

The statue can be serious or funny. Encourage family members to be imaginative. Have the rest of the family guess each pair's listening skill. Encourage people to write the skills in their journals as the pairs explain them. Then ask:

● **What skills seem most natural to you? most difficult?**

● **What skill is our family best at? worst at?**

● **How can we improve the skills we're worst at?**

GO

Have volunteers read aloud the following scriptures: Proverbs 17:28; Proverbs 18:2; Matthew 11:15; Luke 10:38-42; and James 1:19.

Ask:

● **What practical wisdom about listening can we gain from these passages?**

● **Which passage speaks most directly to you? Why?**

At the top of a page in their journals, have people write: "(their name), you were all ears when . . ." Then pass

Five Keys to Great Listening

1. Assume an interested body position. Your body position should tell a person, "I care and am interested in you." Sit beside the person, lean toward him or her, or just be close. Don't fold your arms or do other actions that make you seem uninterested.

2. Maintain eye contact. Eye contact lets the person know you're giving him or her your undivided attention. And it keeps you from getting distracted.

3. Note non-verbal cues. Pick up on the speaker's body language—his or her posture and facial expressions. These clues often tell a lot about how someone feels. When you see a clue, don't assume you understand it. Ask about it. "You look really down today. Is everything okay?"

4. Reflect words and feelings. Restate what the speaker has said so he or she will know you hear and understand. "So you're angry at your teacher because she put you down in front of the whole class."

5. Give non-judgmental responses. Giving advice—"Just dump her"—or dismissing feelings—"You'll get over it"—only hurts people and cuts off communication. Instead, give non-judgmental responses, such as, "That sounds really tough."

everyone's journal around the family. Have family members each write a time when that person really listened to them. Have them specifically praise one listening skill they saw. For example: "James, I really appreciated how you respected my feelings and took me seriously when I told you about my lousy day at work."

When everyone has written in everyone else's journal, have family members each pass their journal to the person across from them. Then ask family members each to thank God for the person whose journal they have, focusing on the ways that person is a good listener.

THE EXTRA MILE

Through the coming week, encourage people to leave "You Were All Ears" affirmation notes for each other. Talk about and practice good listening skills during the week.

WHAT'CHA WATCHIN'?

PURPOSE: To evaluate television's messages and set viewing standards.

MATERIALS: For each family member you'll need a journal, a pencil, a Bible and three 3×5 cards.

PREPARATION: None needed.

GET READY

Begin this devotion by playing Name That Show. Here's how it works: Have family members each think of their three favorite TV shows (current or old). Make sure family members know the shows pretty well so they can give good clues. Have people write the titles in their own journals but not reveal them to anyone else.

Then have one person give clues about his or her show. Pause after each clue to give people time to guess. A clue can be a word from the title, a character's name, the setting, a common expression on the show, a phrase from the theme song—anything that's unique to the show.

Each person can guess only once after each clue. If someone guesses correctly, give him or her one point. If no one guesses, have the person give more clues until someone guesses.

Continue playing until everyone's shows have been guessed. Total the scores, and reward the winner by letting him or her choose the shows the family watches for one day. Ask:

- **What do you like about your favorite shows?**
- **What positive messages have you received from your favorite shows? Describe the scenes.**
- **What negative messages have you received? Describe them.**

GET SET

Have someone read aloud 1 Kings 3:16-28. Say: **When it comes to television, we sometimes feel like Solomon must have felt being pulled between two conflicting views. We need Solomon's insight to make wise choices about what we watch.**

Ask:
- **What similarities do you see between the situation Solomon faced and the choices we make when we watch television?**
- **Solomon found out what was true by probing deeper into the situation. What are some ways we can probe into the shows we view in order to make better decisions?**

GO

On each of three 3×5 cards, have family members each describe a different situation they've seen on television that raised questions related to one of the following issues: sexuality or nudity; violence or lawlessness; glorification of alcohol or drugs; racial, sexist or religious bias; materialism or selfishness; and bad language.

Say: **Now we're going to talk about how we should respond to each situation. When someone reads a situation, immediately indicate your choice with the appropriate hand actions.**

Explain these three options:

1. Leave, switch channels or turn off the television. (Cover your eyes with your hands.)

2. Keep watching as long as the show isn't offensive. Concentrate on the show's redeeming qualities. (Put your hand on your chin as though you're thinking.)

3. Don't worry about it! Enjoy the scenes. (Fold your arms.)

When everyone understands the actions, have each person read his or her situations. After each one, have people do their motions. Discuss differences in what people choose. Discuss how to make wise decisions when confronted with particular scenes on television. Continue until you've discussed all the situations.

Read aloud Philippians 1:9-11. Ask:

● **How can we apply this passage to our television use?**

As a family, think of specific guidelines you'll use in watching television. Agree on what kinds of shows you will and won't watch.

Pray together the prayer that Solomon prayed asking for God's wisdom: "Give your servant a discerning heart . . . to distinguish between right and wrong" (1 Kings 3:9).

THE EXTRA MILE

Look through the TV guide for the coming week, and select two or three shows to watch together as a family. During each show, have each person take notes based on what you learned in this devotion. Afterward, discuss the show in light of your family's guidelines.

TORN APART

PURPOSE: To discuss divorce and ways to help those who've been through it.

MATERIALS: You'll need cellophane tape.

For each family member you'll need a paper towel, a marker, a Bible, a journal and a pencil.

PREPARATION: None needed.

GET READY

Give family members each a paper towel and marker. Have them each draw a picture of a happy family in the center of the towel. When they're finished, have people each hold their towel by the edges and try to tear it exactly in half. Ask:

- **How did you feel as you tore the towel?**
- **How is the uneven tearing similar to or different from divorce?**

GET SET

Assign each person one of the following passages. It's okay for two people to have one passage or for one person to have two passages. Here are the passages: Malachi 2:13-16; Matthew 5:31-32; Matthew 19:3-9; and John 4:4-30.

Have people each read their passage. Then ask:

- **How did Jesus respond to the woman at the well, knowing she'd gone through five husbands and**

now lived with a man? What did Jesus offer her?
- **Why do you think God hates divorce?**
- **What is God's attitude toward divorced people?**
- **How does God respond to divorce today?**

Have people look at their towel pieces from the Get
Ready exercise. Ask:
- **What do you think the jags in the taped-together towels represent?**
- **What does this exercise tell you about the pain of divorce?**

Read aloud John 8:1-11 and 1 Peter 4:8. Ask:
- **How should Christians respond to those who divorce?**
- **What special needs—emotional and spiritual—does a divorced person have?**
- **How can we help families of divorced parents?**

If your family has experienced a divorce, ask:
- **What can we do as a family to ease the healing process?**

Pray that family members will be sensitive to needs of
people who've been affected by a divorce.

THE EXTRA MILE

Imagine your minister has just announced that he or she
is divorcing, but would like to remain the church's minister.
Form two teams to debate the question of whether your
church should consent. During the debate, refer to Deuteronomy 24:1-4; 1 Timothy 3:2; Titus 1:6; and the other passages
in this devotion.

AND THE LAUGH SHALL BE FIRST

PURPOSE: To celebrate God's healing gift of laughter.

MATERIALS: For each family member you'll need a Bible, a journal and a pencil.

PREPARATION: None needed.

GET READY

Have family members sit in a circle. Say: **We're going to see who can keep from laughing the longest.**

It won't take long to discover who can hold out. Congratulate the winner. Explain that this "stone-faced" person now gets to be a "sculpture."

Have the sculpture sit in an open space. Then have other people—the "artists"—take turns sculpting this person. The sculpture should relax and allow each artist to sculpt his or her face and body. The artist's goal is to sculpt the craziest expression and pose. Judge the winner by the sculpture that gets the most laughs.

When the laughter dies down, read aloud Proverbs 17:22. Ask:

● **How have laughter and humor helped our family? Give examples.**

● **When has a good round of laughter brightened your perspective when you were down or depressed?**

GET SET

Say: **Though we don't often think about it, the Bible is filled with funny stories.**

Ask family members to think of examples. Then assign one of the following scriptures to each person: Genesis 18:9-15; 1 Samuel 17:4-16, 34-51; Matthew 5:15; Matthew 7:9-11; Luke 18:23-25; and Acts 20:7-12.

Have people each pretend to be a late-night talk show host and give a short monologue about their passage. When everyone has performed, ask:

● **Was it uncomfortable to laugh about Bible stories and verses? Why or why not?**

● **How was this interpretation of the passage different from the way you've always thought of it? Do you like the difference? Why or why not?**

● **How does seeing humor in the Bible change your perception of God?**

GO

Say: **Some forms of humor are pure fun. But other forms are phony, cynical, biting and distasteful.**

Ask family members to brainstorm differences between healthy and unhealthy humor. Have people each write the ideas in their journals. Ask:

● **When have you been a victim of cruel humor? How did you feel?**

● **What form of humor do you find most offensive? Why?**

● **What forms of humor do you enjoy most? Why?**

● **Are you sometimes tempted to use sick humor? If so, when and why?**

Brainstorm ways to reduce sick humor and increase healthy humor in family life. Close with a group prayer. Encourage all family members to pray, thanking God for a specific time when laughter encouraged them or lifted them up. Pray that God will lead you to healthy humor.

THE EXTRA MILE

Have the family watch a comedy on television. Ask:
- **What made the show funny?**
- **What was the funniest part? Why?**
- **Was the humor at the expense of other people?**

Why or why not?

FIGHT RIGHT

PURPOSE: To help family members gain skills to resolve arguments.

MATERIALS: You'll need a straight pin and seven 3×5 cards.

For each family member you'll need a balloon, a Bible, a journal and a pencil.

PREPARATION: Write each of the guidelines from the first column of the "Fight Right" box on a separate 3×5 card.

GET READY

Give each person a balloon. Say: **Whenever I say "argue" or "argument," blow into your balloon. Whenever I say "relieve," let out some air.**

When everyone's ready, read the following description. Pause after each word in italics. When you read the last sentence, pop everyone's balloon with the pin.

Say: **Whenever we *argue*, pressure builds in the family. That's not usually a problem, if we resolve the *argument* and *relieve* the pressure. But sometimes we have *argument* after *argument*. We *argue* about anything we can think to *argue* about. And we *argue* with everybody there is to *argue* with. So the *arguments* just build on top of other *arguments*. Before long, something happens. And we explode.**

Ask:

● **What feelings did you have when I popped the balloon?**

● **In what areas does our family let conflict build until it explodes?**
● **How can we "let the air out" of our arguments before they explode?**

In their journals, have people each make a blank chart to match the "Fight Right" chart. Lay the "Fight Right" guideline cards upside down on the table. One by one, have each person draw a card and read aloud the guideline. Have people write it in the chart. Then brainstorm together examples to fit the columns. If you're stumped, read the examples in the "Fight Right" box. Continue until you've talked about all the guidelines. Ask:
● **Which guidelines do you most need to develop?**
● **How can you put this guideline into action?**

Go

Leave the "Fight Right" cards on the table. Assign family members each one or more of these scripture passages: Proverbs 12:18; Matthew 5:23-24; Romans 12:17-18; Ephesians 4:29-32; and Colossians 4:6. Have them each think of which guideline or guidelines the passage supports. Then have them read the passage aloud and write the scripture reference on the appropriate "Fight Right" card or cards.

Next work together as a family to create "Fight Right Be-Attitudes." Rewrite each guideline in the format of Christ's beatitudes in Matthew 5:3-10. For example, guideline #5 could become: "Blessed are those who forgive and forget, for they shall enjoy peace with God and each other." Have family members write the new versions in their journals. Close with prayer, asking God for wisdom and humility to resolve conflicts according to his will and Word.

Fight Right

Guideline	Inappropriate Response	Appropriate Response
1. Use "I" statements, not "you" statements.	"You make me mad when you don't listen to me."	"I get angry when I feel you're not listening."
2. Avoid "never" and "always" statements.	"You never do anything I ask you to do!"	"I really need your help with this project."
3. Listen to the other person.	"That reminds me that I need to buy gas for the lawn mower."	"So you're saying you already have plans?"
4. Attack the problem, not the person.	"You're crazy to think you can do all that."	"I'm not sure anyone can do that much."
5. Avoid "throwing snowballs" from previous arguments.	"I'm fed up with you! Yesterday you didn't take out the trash. Today you didn't trim the grass. What next?"	"Will you be able to cut the grass today?"
6. Watch your tone and volume.	"Shut up! I've had it with you!"	"I need to calm down before we talk."
7. Cool off before you confront.	"I've had a rough day, and now you're asking me to help you!? You're so inconsiderate."	"I'm really frazzled right now. Give me an hour to rest before we talk about it."

THE EXTRA MILE

Think of a crazy, made-up word, such as "boink" or "hanya," to use as a "pressure detector" during the coming week. When someone hears a family member not following the "Fight Right" guidelines, he or she says the word. It's a good reminder and helps defuse a tense situation.

DRESS DISTRESS

PURPOSE: To explore biblical principles for dress and appearance.

MATERIALS: You'll need recent clothing catalogs.

For each family member you'll need a Bible, a journal and a pencil.

PREPARATION: None needed.

GET READY

Have family members each look through clothing catalogs to find one outfit that represents typical dress for each of the following groups: teenagers, young adults, middle-aged adults and elderly adults. Have people each explain their choices. Ask:

● **Why do people wear what they wear?**

● **Why is there sometimes tension between generations about dress?**

● **Does a person's clothing send messages? Give examples.**

GET SET

Assign each family member one or more of the following verses. Some of the passages are addressed just to women or men. Treat them as speaking to either gender. Here are the verses: Proverbs 31:10, 24-25; Matthew 6:28-34; Luke 3:10-14; 1 Timothy 2:9-10; James 2:1-4; and 1 Peter 3:3-4.

In their journal, have family members each write:

● how the passage applies to appearance and dress; and

● a few guidelines for dressing based on the passage.

Ask family members each to read their passage and share insights. Discuss these as a family. Have people keep notes in their journals.

Are You What You Wear?

Situation #1—Shelly believes God's children should wear the best clothes because it impresses non-believers. She feels that a lot of people think you have to be boring to be a Christian, and she's just trying to set the record straight by always wearing the latest styles. How do you feel about Shelly's ideas?

Situation #2—Brian's family can't afford expensive clothes, but Brian doesn't want to look different from his friends. Brian's friends harass him a lot about the way he dresses. Brian and his parents have had a big fight over an expensive pair of tennis shoes Brian wants. How do you think Brian feels? What's he thinking? What should his parents do?

Situation #3—Christine just bought a swimsuit that reveals a lot more of Christine than her mother will allow. Her mother wants her to get a more modest swimsuit. What advice would you give Christine? What would you say to her mother?

Situation #4—Stanley's family believes Christians should dress simply so they'll have more money to give away. Stanley agrees, but he often feels out-of-place at school—and even at church—where other people wear nice, fashionable clothes. How should Stanley deal with the situation and his feelings?

Read aloud the "Are You What You Wear?" situations and apply the scriptural principles you discovered in the Get Set section. Then ask:

● **What's our family's philosophy of how we dress?**

● **What are potential family conflict areas about clothing? How can we deal with these issues so the**

problem doesn't explode?

● **How can we support and encourage each other in our choices?**

Ask family members each to select one item of clothing that will represent their commitment to keep a biblical perspective on what they wear. For example, someone might choose shoes and say, "I'll stand firm when people criticize what I wear." Have people each show their item and say why they chose it. Close by reading 1 Peter 6:13-18.

THE EXTRA MILE

Take a family trip to a shopping mall and look at the latest fashions. Discuss how important clothing is to each family member as well as why people each wear what they wear. Notice the differences and similarities between the reasons teenagers and parents choose their clothes.

YOU'RE THE GREATEST

PURPOSE: To give family members an opportunity to affirm each other.

MATERIALS: You'll need cellophane tape and paper.

For each family member you'll need a household item, a journal, a pencil and a Bible.

PREPARATION: Gather a household item for each person. Suggested items: toilet paper, paper plate, pot-holder, sponge, soap, empty bottle, rubber band, spatula or cup.

GET READY

Have everyone sit in a circle, and place the household items in the center. Ask people each to choose an item, beginning with the person who got up first this morning and ending with you.

Allow two minutes for family members each to think of all the "selling strengths" of their item and to write them in their journal. For example, someone might write that one selling strength of a paper plate is that it's disposable. Then have people read their lists of benefits and uses. Ask:

● **What was it like to think of all the good things about your item?**

● **Do you think it would be easier to think of all the problems with your item? Why or why not?**

● **When was a time you concentrated on finding all the good points in another person? What was that experience like for you?**

● **Why do you think we don't often affirm people?**

Read aloud the following passages and discuss the questions together:

- Ephesians 4:29-32—What percentage of all the conversations you hear daily build people up? Why do you think that is?
- Philippians 2:1-4—What aspects of Christ's attitude toward others would you most like to develop? Why?
- Hebrews 3:13—How can encouraging a family member or friend keep that person's heart from becoming hard?
- Hebrews 10:24-25—How much do you actively encourage family members and friends?

On a piece of paper, have family members each draw a "Strength Banner" (see sample) and tape it to their back. In-

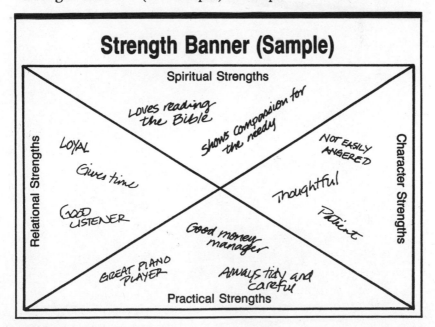

vite other family members to write words of affirmation on each other's banner.

When everyone is ready, have people read their banners. Then ask them each to give their banner to someone else. Form a circle and have a family member kneel in the center of the circle.

Ask the person who's holding the kneeler's banner to thank God for the strengths in that person. Use the banner for ideas. Repeat the process until everyone has been in the center. Close by thanking God for bringing such wonderful people together in your family.

THE EXTRA MILE

Give family members each an envelope to decorate and tape to their bedroom door. Encourage people to drop affirmation notes to each other in the envelopes through the coming week. They can affirm something the person did or something they appreciate about the person.

ROOTS

PURPOSE: To explore your family history.

MATERIALS: You'll need markers and a medium-size cardboard box.

For each family member you'll need a journal, a pencil and a Bible.

PREPARATION: None needed.

GET READY

Show everyone the "Coat of Arms" below. Have family members each sketch a similar coat of arms in their journal. Then read aloud what they're to put in each box, pausing to allow family members to write. When you finish, have people share what they wrote.

Ask:
- **Which part of your coat of arms do you feel most strongly about?**
- **How did you feel while filling out your coat of arms?**

Coat of Arms

My full name:	I was named after:
Two strengths my father gave me:	Two strengths my mother gave me:
Two relatives who've made the strongest impression on me—besides Mom and Dad:	The part of my family heritage that I'm most proud of is:
The best part about being in this family is:	Concerning my family history, I'm most thankful for:
The two family traits I would most like to see passed down to future generations are:	
My main reason for living is:	

Assign one of these verses to each family member: Exodus 20:5-6; Psalm 78:2-7; and Psalm 112:1-3. Ask:

● **In what ways has your faith been passed down to you?**

● **What would you like to be remembered for by your descendants?**

Display a medium-size cardboard box and say: **We're going to create a family time-capsule. Let's gather personal objects and other items that describe the times we live in now. Then we'll store the capsule and look at it again in five years.**

Have family members gather items for the time capsule. Suggest pages from today's newspaper, recent photographs of each family member, a list of favorite TV shows or movies, or a list of each family member's top five concerns.

After the time capsule is loaded, dated, and sealed with tape, have family members use markers to decorate it with drawings of things they value in their lives.

Store the capsule in a dry place. Then pray together for God to keep your family close. Thank God for your family heritage and each person's contribution to it.

THE EXTRA MILE

Prepare a meal together that features food common to the land of your family's ancestors. Consider donning native costumes for the event. Enjoy!

DON'T INVADE MY SPACE

PURPOSE: To discuss kids' need for increasing independence.

MATERIALS: You'll need four pieces of paper, cellophane tape, and relaxing instrumental music.

For each family member you'll need a marker, a Bible, a journal and a pencil.

PREPARATION: Tape the four pieces of paper together.

GET READY

Gather everyone around a table. Set out the four taped pieces of paper and markers. Play relaxing instrumental music. While the music plays, have family members draw on the paper pictures or symbols that represent independence. For example, someone might draw a bird in flight, broken chains or fireworks. Have people also write words or phrases they associate with independence, such as freedom or liberty. Allow them to continue until the song is over. Then have family members each explain their drawings. Ask:
- **What does "independence" mean to you?**
- **What would be ideal independence for you?**

GET SET

Read aloud Galatians 5:13-14. Then ask:
- **Do you feel Christianity restricts your free-**

dom? Why or why not?

● **How do we sometimes use our freedom in the household to take advantage of others?**

Have volunteers read aloud Hebrews 11:8-10.

● **How do you think Abraham felt when God told him to leave his father's house to face the unknown?**

● **How is this similar to a teenager growing up and moving away from home?**

Have family members each list in their journal the freedoms they want the family's teenagers to have one year, two years and three years from now. They might list freedoms such as driving the car, dating, going on out-of-town trips or finding an apartment. Have family members each share their list. Note differences between kids' and parents' lists. Then ask:

● **What attitude should we have concerning the areas where our opinions differ?**

● **How can these differing opinions be reconciled?**

Sample Family Contract

In order to honor the individual privacy, personal space and independence of each family member, we the Kochenburger family do hereby agree to the following rules of privacy for each member of our household:

1. We'll not read other's mail or notes without permission.

2. We'll knock before entering another person's room.

3. We'll not listen in on other's phone conversations without permission.

4. When out for the evening, we'll always call to let others know where we are and whether we'll be late.

5. We'll not rummage through another person's bedroom.

6. We . . .

Name   Date

_____

_____

_____

_____

Say: **Respecting another person's independence involves recognizing his or her right to privacy. The contract we'll now create together will provide specific guidelines for respecting each person's privacy.**

Read aloud the "Sample Family Contract" on page 106. Then work together to write your own family contract. Adjust the rules to fit your family. Then have each family member sign the contract.

Display the contract in a prominent place in your home, such as your kitchen or family room.

Close with prayer.

THE EXTRA MILE

Have parents write a letter to their teenagers about how they feel knowing they must "let go" of their teenagers. Also have teenagers write a letter to the parents describing their feelings about being out on their own.

WHEN TRAGEDY STRIKES

PURPOSE: To discuss family members' responses to tragedy.

MATERIALS: For each family member you'll need a paper clip, a Bible, a journal and a pencil.

PREPARATION: None needed.

GET READY

Give each family member a paper clip. Have family members each bend their paper clip to form a sculpture in response to the question: When you talk about tragedy, such as a plane crash, death or terminal illness, how do you feel?

Have the family discuss their paper-clip sculptures and their feelings. Then ask:
- **What makes tragedy so painful?**
- **What's your first reaction to tragedy? Explain.**
- **What's the worst thing you could imagine happening to you? Explain.**

GET SET

Have a different family member read aloud each situation in the "Tragic Situations" box. After each is read, have family members say how they'd react in that situation. Then

Tragic Situations

Situation #1: You're a wealthy rancher. You lose all your children and cattle in a single day. You're then afflicted with agonizing diseases. How do you react?

Read Job 1:1-4, 13-19 and 20-22.

Situation #2: Your own family despises you. The only one with any love for you is your dad. Your other family members hate you so much they sell you into slavery. How do you react?

Read Genesis 37:23-28; and 45:1-8.

Situation #3: You commit a serious sin. To cover it up you have a friend murdered. You get caught. How do you react?

Read 2 Samuel 12:1-14 and 15-20.

read aloud the Bible passages under that situation. Ask:

● **How did your response differ from the biblical character's in the same situation?**

● **What do these passages tell us about tragedy?**

Have family members brainstorm ways to respond compassionately to those who suffer tragedy. Have family members write their ideas in their journals. Then work as a family to form a "Compassion Task Force" in your church. Enlist concerned adults and kids to visit tragedy-stricken families and do for them some of the things your family suggested. Make this an ongoing ministry in your church.

THE EXTRA MILE

To help family members understand what it's like to suffer personal physical tragedy, have them go 12 hours with one of these conditions: with a blindfold; with ear plugs; without speaking; or without walking.

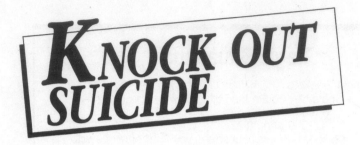

KNOCK OUT SUICIDE

PURPOSE: To discuss suicide and discover ways to prevent it.

MATERIALS: For each family member you'll need a journal, a pencil and a Bible.

PREPARATION: None needed.

GET READY

Have family members take this quiz to check their knowledge of suicide. In their journals, have them each number from one to seven. Read aloud each statement below and have family members each write "T" or "F" depending on whether they believe the statement is true or false. The answers are listed below.

1. Females commit suicide more often than males.

2. More females attempt suicide than males.

3. Only depressed people commit suicide.

4. The elderly have a high suicide rate.

5. Many people who commit suicide have attempted suicide in the past.

6. The highest suicide rate is among the poor, particularly those with little hope of ever rising out of poverty.

7. Every 20 to 30 minutes, someone in the United States takes his or her own life.

Answers: 1. *False.* Males commit suicide three times more frequently than females; **2.** *True.* But males use more violent means of suicide than females and are therefore more likely to complete the suicide; **3.** *False.* Though many suicide victims have just come out of a depression; **4.** *True;* **5.** *True.* About four out of five people who commit suicide have attempted suicide before; **6.** *False.* Suicide is represented proportionately among all socioeconomic levels; **7.** *True.* More than 20,000 people kill themselves each year.

Discuss surprising statements from the quiz. Then ask:

● **How do you feel discussing suicide?**

● **What do you feel drives people your age to commit suicide?**

Read aloud the statements in the "Four to Live For!" box. Have family members each copy them in their journals as you read. Then have family members each circle their top four reasons to live.

Four to Live For

1. Because God loves me—John 3:16
2. The people I love—1 John 2:10
3. God's plan for me—John 10:10
4. My church/youth group—1 Corinthians 12:27
5. My family—Exodus 20:12
6. My spouse or "steady"—Song of Songs 8:6
7. Life is fun—Ecclesiastes 3:12-13
8. The beautiful world—Psalm 19:1-6
9. Chance to serve others—Matthew 20:26

10. I'm loved—1 John 4:7
11. I'm happy—Psalm 68:3
12. My friends—Proverbs 17:17
13. My money/possessions—Luke 12:15
14. Chance to share Christ—Colossians 4:5-6
15. Exciting future—Psalm 23:5-6
16. Because I'm important—Psalm 139:13-16
17. Other_____
_____

Have family members each share the four reasons they circled and read aloud the verses associated with their choices. Then ask:

● **Why did you choose the reasons you did?**

● **With so many reasons to live, why do people still commit suicide?**

Read aloud the following situations. After each situation, assign parts and have family members role-play a conclusion. Have them begin the role play where the case study leaves off. Instruct players to continue until they reach a conclusion or a "stone wall."

Situation #1: Sally recently broke up with her boyfriend. You also know she didn't make the cheerleading squad this year because she got caught with drugs at a football game last season. She's been feeling down a lot lately, and yesterday she said she thought she'd be better off dead.

Situation #2: Bill, your longtime business partner, hasn't been the same since his wife left him for a younger man last month. You've noticed him drinking lately, though you don't remember him ever drinking before. He has lamented that he doesn't see much reason to go on living.

After family members role-play the conclusions, ask:

● **What was good about how each situation was handled?**

● **What are other ways each situation could've been approached?**

Have the family join hands and pray for each other. Have them pray that each one would remind other family members of the abundant life Christ promises.

THE EXTRA MILE

Rent the video called "The Question" (Mars Hill Productions) and watch it as a family. The video tells the story of a young man's suicide. The video is 36 minutes long, but will require at least another 30 minutes for discussion.

CHEERFUL GIVERS

PURPOSE: To look at tithing as a family.

MATERIALS: For each family member you'll need a journal, a pencil, a Bible, a bar of soap and a butter knife.

PREPARATION: None needed.

GET READY

Have family members each write in their journal a gift they'd give to each family member. Tell them they have unlimited resources to draw from for their gift. Then have them each find an object to represent each gift and give it to the appropriate family member. For example, if someone wanted to give a mansion, he or she could give a door key.
Have family members explain their gifts. Then ask:

- **What's fun about giving?**
- **Why is it sometimes hard to give?**
- **What are the hardest things for you to give?**

GET SET

Read aloud the situations from the "Giving Situations" box. For each situation ask:

- **Is this a good or bad giving attitude? Why?**

Assign one of the following Bible passages to each person: Matthew 6:1-4; Mark 12:41-44; and 2 Corinthians 9:6-7. Have family members each draw in their journal a picture of what the verses describe. Then have them each read aloud their scripture and explain their drawing.

● **What's the most important attitude to have when giving?**

● **Is it okay for Christians to be rich? Why or why not?**

Giving Situations

1. John gives money to the church because he's afraid of what others would think if he didn't.

2. Sarah gives to the TV ministry she watches because the evangelist cries during the plea for money, and she feels sorry for him.

3. Jamie tithes because he feels it's his privilege as a Christian.

4. Sue tithes every week. She also gives to the poor through the local relief agency. She feels everything she owns is on loan from the Lord.

Give each person a bar of soap and a butter knife. Have them each "sculpt" something out of the soap that represents giving. For example, they might sculpt a hand with coins in it or a cross.

When everyone is finished, ask family members each to explain their sculpture. Then say: **Keep these sculptures in the bathroom so we'll be reminded of this devotion every time we shower!**

Close with prayer, asking God to help your family give their money, time and gifts to build God's kingdom.

THE EXTRA MILE

Have family members each list their most valued possessions in order according to importance. Pray together over the lists, offering each item to God—acknowledging his ownership of all that we have.

MONEY MATTERS

PURPOSE: To discuss family finances from a biblical perspective.

MATERIALS: You'll need a rubber ball.

For each family member you'll need a Bible, a journal and a pencil.

PREPARATION: None needed.

GET READY

Read "The Great Giveaway" aloud. Have family members answer the question at the end. Then read the answer.

The Great Giveaway

Once upon a time there was a wealthy man who had twin sons. The man was deciding which son should take over the family business. So he summoned his sons and said, "I'd like to give you a large sum of money and I'm offering you a choice of two ways to receive it. You may take a check from me for $1 million right now. Or take this penny from me now, and tomorrow I'll give you two pennies. The next day I'll give you four pennies. Each day for 30 days I'll double what I gave you the day before. Which one do you choose?"

The first son quickly took the $1 million check. The other son chose the penny. Which son became richer and the heir to his father's business?

Answer: The son who took the penny won. His fortune totaled over $10 million! His brother got only $1 million.

Ask:

● **Which son in the story do you most resemble? Explain.**

● **Do you feel you handle money wisely? Why or why not?**

Assign each of these scriptures to a family member: Proverbs 11:24-25; Matthew 6:24; Luke 12:31-34; and 1 John 3:17. Hold up a rubber ball and say: **Read your verse aloud and then use this rubber ball to illustrate the passage.**

Have family members each read their passage and illustrate it with the ball. For example, for Proverbs 11:24-25 a family member could bounce the ball to indicate how the generous man gives things away, yet receives things back. Then ask:

● **What can we learn about our finances from these scriptures?**

Say: **With good planning we can all spend our money more wisely. At the top of a blank page in your journal, write the total amount you receive each month. Then divide your sheet into two columns. I'll read a series of budget items. Copy each one into the left column in your journal.**

Read aloud this list, pausing between each item to allow family members to write:

- Church and charity
- Housing costs
- Clothes
- Telephone and utilities
- Entertainment
- Education and self-improvement
- Savings and investments
- Food
- Car
- Insurance
- Hobbies
- Pocket money

After everyone has finished writing, say: **In the second column, next to each budget item, put the amount you spend each month in that area. If a budget item doesn't apply to you, just ignore it. Be honest.**

When everyone is finished, ask:

- **What surprised you most about your budget?**
- **What would you like to change about the way you handle money?**
- **What steps can you take to make that happen?**

Pray that family members would give God control of their finances, and that you would honor God as a family in the way you handle money.

THE EXTRA MILE

Have your teenagers help pay the family bills this month. Explain your family's monthly budget, and have your teenagers write out the checks to help understand where the money goes.

MATERIAL WORLD

PURPOSE: To examine the effects of materialism.

MATERIALS: For each family member you'll need a Bible, a journal and a pencil.

PREPARATION: None needed.

GET READY

Read aloud the following poem.

Richard Cory

Whenever Richard Cory went
  down town,
We people on the pavement
  looked at him:
He was a gentleman from sole to
  crown,
Clean favored, and imperially
  slim.

And he was always quietly arrayed,
And he was always human when
  he talked;
But still he fluttered pulses when
  he said,
'Good-morning,' and he glittered
  when he walked.

And he was rich—yes, richer than
  a king—
And admirably schooled in every
  grace:
In fine, we thought that he was
  everything
To make us wish that we were in
  his place.

So on we worked, and waited for
  the light,
And went without the meat, and
  cursed the bread;
And Richard Cory, one calm
  summer night,
Went home and put a bullet
  through his head.

Ask:
- **Materially, Richard Cory had it all. Why would he take his life?**
- **Why is it sometimes easier to trust in money than in God?**

Read aloud the following statements. After you read each statement, have family members each stand up if they agree with the statement or remain seated if they disagree. Have them explain why they responded as they did.

- It isn't right to buy expensive things or things you don't really need while other people suffer and have nothing.
- Being rich or having more than you absolutely need shows God's blessing and favor to you. Also, being poor is a result of not pleasing God.
- It's possible to be materialistic, yet have few material goods.
- Americans should feel guilty for having so much when people from other countries have so little.

Ask:
- **What problems are caused by living in a materialistic society?**
- **How do you think people in other nations feel when they see our standard of living?**

Go

Assign someone to read aloud each of the following verses. After each is read, have family members respond to the questions and statements that follow.

- 1 Timothy 6:10—Can someone be poor and still be ruled by a love for money? What bad things can happen to someone because of money?

● 1 Samuel 2:7-8—Come up with five reasons we should look to God rather than money to meet our needs.

● Matthew 6:24—Why can't someone serve two masters at the same time?

Read aloud Matthew 6:19-21. Have family members each draw a treasure chest in their journal, and title it "My Earthly Treasure." Then have them each draw another treasure chest and title it "My Heavenly Treasure."

Say: **It's a miracle! God has blessed you by allowing you to see both your heavenly treasure and your Earthly treasure. First open your Earthly treasure chest. Below the treasure chest write all you see. You have one minute.**

Examples could be cars, money, clothes or music.

After one minute, say: **Now look into your heavenly treasure chest and write what you see in there! You have one minute.**

Examples could be fellowship with God or close friendships.

● **How did your treasures compare?**

● **Which have you really been investing in— heavenly or Earthly treasure?**

Say: **In your journal, write four things you can do to build more treasure in heaven than on Earth.** For example, coordinate a ministry project to children, the elderly or your family; support a needy child in a foreign land; or begin a regular time of Bible study and prayer each day.

Thank the Lord for the treasure found in Christ. Pray that your family would become free from materialism and would instead invest in eternal treasures.

THE EXTRA MILE

As a family, look at the four things you wrote from the Go section, and choose one to begin to do together.

ALL RACES ONE

PURPOSE: To show how prejudice hurts and offer ways to avoid it.

MATERIALS: You'll need a pan of brownies or cookies, a slice of stale bread and a piece of paper.

For each family member you'll need a Bible, a paper towel tube or bathroom tissue tube, a journal and a pencil.

PREPARATION: Prepare brownies or cookies for this devotion. Also set out a slice of bread a few hours before devotion time so it will become stale.

GET READY

Give all but one person a brownie or cookie. Give the extra person a slice of stale bread. Don't allow those with brownies or cookies to share their treats. After everyone has finished eating, ask the person who got stale bread:

● **How did it feel to receive stale bread while everyone around you got sweets?**

● **How did this exercise make you feel about yourself?**

Now ask everyone:

● **How is this like prejudice?**

● **What kinds of prejudice do you encounter?**

Give the extra person a brownie or cookie.

GET SET

Divide a piece of paper into eight sections. One by one,

draw in the sections the steps shown in the "Step After Step" box. After drawing each step, let each person guess what it is. Keep drawing until someone guesses correctly.

Then ask:

● **Why was it hard to identify the picture at first?**

● **How is that like stereotyping people because of their color, sex, heritage or income?**

Have volunteers read aloud Acts 10:34-35 and Galatians 3:26-29. Ask:

● **Concerning favoritism, how can we demonstrate an attitude like God's?**

● **How is being "clothed" with Christ a uniting bond between different races, sexes and income levels?**

● **How should we respond to the prejudice around us?**

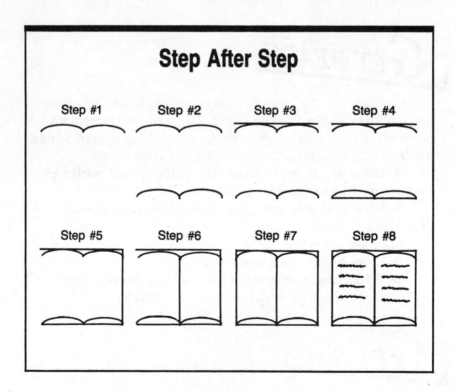

Step After Step

Step #1 Step #2 Step #3 Step #4

Step #5 Step #6 Step #7 Step #8

Give each person a paper towel tube or bathroom tissue tube. Have family members sit close together and look at each other through their tubes. Have family members each write in their journal how others are different from them.

Say: **Prejudice is like looking through this tube at one another. We see little of the person and make a decision about them. We also tend to dwell on the differences between us rather than on the similarities.**

Ask:

● **How is prejudice unfair and damaging?**

● **Can you think of any prejudices you have? Explain.**

Have the family pray together that prejudice would not blind any family member. Also pray that family members each would know what it means to be clothed with Christ in their daily walk with God.

THE EXTRA MILE

Each week for the next few months, set aside one meal as a "global" meal. Choose a different culture each week, such as Chinese or Jewish, and serve foods common to that culture. As you eat, talk about the things you appreciate about that culture.

STRESS MESS

PURPOSE: To help family members overcome stress.

MATERIALS: You'll need a "Nose for the News" award.

For each family member you'll need a newspaper, a Bible, a journal and a pencil.

PREPARATION: Create a "Nose for the News" award like the drawing below. Just copy the drawing onto a piece of paper.

GET READY

Give each family member a newspaper. Have family members look for each of the items in the "Nose for the News" box. No article or ad can be used for more than one

---

Nose for the News

Find:
- an article in the sports section that mentions money.
- an article on crime in your town.
- an ad for a car that's 10 years old or older.
- an article that mentions the President of the United States.
- an ad for drapery cleaning.
- an article that reports someone's death.
- an article about illegal drugs.
- an article that describes a tragedy.
- an article that deals with abortion, gay rights or prejudice.

item. Have family members tear out their articles and ads. The family member who finds the most items in five minutes gets the official "Nose for the News" award. Ask:

● **How much stress do news issues cause you? Explain.**

● **Do you agree with the statement, "No news is good news"? Why or why not?**

● **What in your life is currently causing you stress?**

Say: **When stress isn't handled correctly, it can cause physical and spiritual harm. Physically, stress causes blood vessels to constrict, resulting in headaches and other pains. Stress can also lead to ulcers and nervous disorders. Spiritually, stress can undermine your peace and joy, causing frustration and hopelessness.**

Have family members pantomime their responses to the following potential stressors. Encourage them to be as realistic as possible. Here are the stressors:

● It's noon and you discover you forgot to use deodorant.

● You have a big pimple on your nose.

● You discover you'll have to move in a few weeks.

● You'll be married in one hour.

● You're going to the dentist.

● A close friend just died.

● You're passed over for a big promotion; or you didn't make the team.

After the pantomimes, ask:

● **Which of these situations would cause you the most stress?**

● **Do you handle stress well? Why or why not?**

Go

Have volunteers read aloud each of these scripture passages, and discuss how they apply to stress management: Matthew 6:34; Luke 12:22-34; Romans 8:28; and Philippians 4:6-9. Have family members each record their insights in their journal. Then ask:

● **How does faith in God help you manage stress?**
● **What can you do to put these scriptures to work in your life?**

Pray that family members would cast their anxieties on Christ and learn to walk in God's peace.

THE EXTRA MILE

Set aside an evening this week to go out as a family and do nothing but have fun! Maybe see a play or a movie, or go to a sports park or playground. Don't talk about the stressful things in your life. Just relax and have a good time!

BAD NEWS BOOZE

PURPOSE: To discuss alcohol abuse from a biblical perspective.

MATERIALS: You'll need paper and cellophane tape.

For each family member you'll need a journal, a pencil, a marker and a Bible.

PREPARATION: None needed.

GET READY

Have family members each list in their journal what they see as the top five reasons people their age use alcohol. Have family members explain their lists. As they share, list all the reasons on one piece of paper.

Tape two pieces of paper together to create a mini-billboard. Brainstorm anti-alcohol-abuse slogans based on the list of reasons people abuse alcohol. For example, if someone listed "peer pressure," your anti-abuse slogan could be "Don't give in to 'high' pressure!" Give everyone a marker and have family members write the slogans on the billboard. Encourage them to decorate the billboard. Then ask:

- **What media messages persuade people to drink alcohol?**
- **What negative effects of alcohol use are left out of alcohol advertisements?**
- **How can we get our billboard's message across to others?**

GET SET

Have family members each draw five beer-bottle shapes on one page in their journal. Have them write one of the following scripture references in each bottle: Proverbs 20:1; Proverbs 23:19-21; John 2:1-11; Romans 14:17-21; and Galatians 5:19-21. Have them each write in each bottle what guidance that Bible passage offers for alcohol use.

Have family members share what they wrote. Then read aloud Ephesians 5:18 and ask:

- **What does "filled with the Spirit" mean to you?**
- **Why is being filled with the Spirit better than being drunk?**

GO

As a family, create a Family Alcohol Pact. On a piece of paper, write how your family will view alcohol use and how you'll respond when it's being abused. Use these questions to help you discuss your opinions:

- How will you help a friend who has a drinking problem?
- How will you respond to those who pressure you to use alcohol?
- Should parents and teenagers have the same restrictions on their alcohol use? Why or why not?

Have each family member sign and date the pact. Close by having family members pray that they'd be filled with the Spirit and not influenced by alcohol.

THE EXTRA MILE

Help your teenager plan a non-alcoholic party to show how easy it is to have a good time without alcohol.

LIFE PARTNERS

PURPOSE: To explore the meaning of marriage.

MATERIALS: You'll need 30 3×5 cards.

For each family member you'll need a Bible, a journal and a pencil.

PREPARATION: Make two identical sets of 15 3×5 cards by writing each of these good marriage qualities on two separate 3×5 cards: 100 percent commitment, unselfishness, sacrifice, openness, common interests, love, patience, willingness to change, sense of humor, trust, communication, respect, thoughtfulness, shared values, and honesty.

GET READY

Have the family members each find an item that represents marriage. When people return, have them each explain their item. Then have family members discuss how the following items are like or unlike marriage: a metal alloy; a feast; a "doubles" tennis team; two halves of a dollar bill; a business partnership; and an adventure. Ask:
- **What's the best part of being married? the worst part?**
- **What's most essential to a good marriage?**

GET SET

Shuffle together the two sets of cards. Place the cards face down in six rows of five cards each. This game is a lot like the old game Concentration and is played like this: Family members take turns turning over two cards to see if they can get a match—two identical cards. Every time a person gets a match, he or she keeps those two cards and receives 100 points. If a person doesn't get a match, he or she turns the cards back over and the next player starts his or her turn. Each player's turn continues until that person fails to get a match. Let the person with the longest name start.

When everyone is finished, add the scores to see who's ahead. Then take one set of the cards and stack them face down. You should have 15 cards. Flip the top card and see who can find a scripture to support this quality. The first one to find a scripture and read it aloud gets 100 points.

After going through all 15 cards, total the scores and award the winner one of these prizes: no chores for a day; night out with friends; or a favorite dinner. Ask:

● **Why do you think so many marriages fail?**

● **The Bible speaks of marriage as a covenant. What does that mean?**

● **What makes you a good person to marry?**

Join hands, thanking God for marriage and its blessings.

THE EXTRA MILE

Parents, talk about your marriage day. Tell how you felt at the time and how you feel now. Explain what the commitment of marriage means. Have your teenagers also share their insights into what marriage is like.

FAMILY FLAVORS

PURPOSE: To help family members understand each other's personality.

MATERIALS: You'll need a grocery sack, assorted items, a package of 3×5 cards and cellophane tape.

For each family member you'll need a Bible, a journal, a pencil and a wire coat hanger.

PREPARATION: Into a grocery sack place the assorted items such as: a piece of fruit, a jar with a lid, a rock, a tiny pillow, a newspaper ad, a piece of candy, an "I love you" note, a "Let me out" note in a sandwich bag, a greeting card, a poem or a book of poetry, a peanut, a mirror and a sock.

GET READY

Form a circle. Pass the grocery sack around, and have each person pull an item out of the bag. Then have each person complete the sentence: "This item is like or unlike my personality because . . ." Repeat the process one or two times, allowing family members to draw new objects from the bag. Then ask:

● **Which item from your selection most accurately represents you? Explain.**

● **Is it easy for you to describe yourself to others? Why or why not?**

Have family members each read these scriptures: Psalm 139:1-6; Romans 15:5-7; and Philippians 4:8. After reading each scripture, have family members each write a response to this question in their journal: What does this scripture say about relating to other family members? When everyone is finished, discuss what family members discovered.

Give everyone a wire hanger. Have family members each draw a "picture" of their personality on a blank page in their journal. For example, someone with an outgoing personality might draw a sun or a big smile. Have them each tear it out and tape it to their hanger.

Open the book to the "Personality Traits" box and lay the book out so everyone can see it. Have family members use the "Personality Traits" box to help them choose which personality traits best describe each person. Family members can also come up with traits not listed in the box. Give family members each a stack of 3×5 cards.

Then have family members complete each mobile by writing out each person's traits on cards and taping them to the appropriate mobile. People can work on every mobile except their own.

Personality Traits

- warm
- extroverted
- strong
- selfless
- determined
- thoughtful
- conservative
- willing

- friendly
- playful
- independent
- pressured
- creative
- sensitive
- practical
- peaceable

- energetic
- withdrawn
- organized
- pessimistic
- quiet
- easygoing
- passive
- liberal

- optimistic
- expressive
- self-confident
- successful
- emotional
- dependable
- loyal

After all the traits have been attached, have people each list in their journal what's on their mobile.

Ask:

● **What surprises you most about your mobile? Explain.**

● **What trait are you the most happy with? least happy? Explain.**

● **What traits do you disagree with or want to clarify?**

Close with prayer, asking God to help family members see themselves as unique and special gifts from God. Also pray that each person would look for the good in others.

*T*HE EXTRA MILE

Have your pastor recommend a comprehensive personality test you can give all family members. Have family members take the test, then evaluate the results together to gain insight into each other's personality.

FRIENDS OF THE FAMILY

PURPOSE: To examine the elements of friendship.

MATERIALS: You'll need several old magazines and newspapers, and cellophane tape.

For each family member you'll need a Bible, a journal and a pencil.

PREPARATION: None needed.

GET READY

Provide old magazines, newspapers and tape. Have family members tear out words and pictures that illustrate friendship. Have them each tape these to one or two pages in their journal. Allow five minutes for family members to complete their collages. Then have them each explain their collage.

GET SET

Say: **One of the greatest friendships in the Bible was between David and Jonathan. Let's take a look at what made that friendship so special.**

Assign each person one of these scriptures and its corresponding friendship quality: 1 Samuel 18:1 (committed love); 1 Samuel 18:4 (willingness to sacrifice); 1 Samuel 19:1-3 (loyalty); 1 Samuel 20:12-13 (trustworthiness); and 1 Samuel 23:15-18 (encouragement). Have family members each read their scripture and explain why that quality is essential to friendship.

Have family members each write in their journal the five qualities of friendship you've discussed. Have family members rate each quality (1=most important to me; 5=least important to me). Have them explain their answers.

Then have people each grade themselves with A, B, C, D or F beside each quality in their journal. Ask:

- **How many of your grades were C or below?**
- **What can you do to improve those areas?**

Say: **Draw a line down the middle of a blank page in your journal. At the top on the left, write "Ad #1." On the right, write "Ad #2."**

In small letters under Ad #1, write "Unbeatable Friendship Offer." In this column, write an ad to interest others in becoming friends with you. Write all the good qualities you have to offer as a friend.

Under Ad #2, write "Looking for a Friend." In this column, write an ad describing what type of friend you'd like to have.

Once everyone is finished, have family members read their ads. After everyone has shared, ask:

- **Which ad was harder to write? Why?**
- **What makes a friendship good?**

Close by having family members thank God for specific close friendships they enjoy.

THE EXTRA MILE

Have family members each write a letter this week to one or two special friends, thanking them for specific things that make them special.

HOME IMPROVEMENTS

PURPOSE: To target family strengths and weaknesses.

MATERIALS: You'll need an instant-print camera or camcorder, and a 12-month calendar.

For each family member you'll need a journal, a pencil and a Bible.

PREPARATION: None needed.

GET READY

Take instant-print pictures of or videotape family members' responses to these contrived situations:

- Teenager wrecks the car—picture parent and teenager.
- Mom's pregnant . . . again—picture Mom.
- Teenager gets home late from a date—picture parent and teenager.
- Dad fixes a leaking drain pipe—picture Dad.

Make up three or four other situations to fit your family. Then ask:

- **What makes our family special? Name our good qualities.**
- **What about our family are you proudest of?**

GET SET

Have family members each draw 10 targets on a page in their journal.

Sample Target

Have family members number their targets one to 10. Then read aloud the numbered items in the "Family Strengths" box. After you read each item, have family members each mark the corresponding numbered target in their journal according to how they feel the family does in that area. The targets are scored as follows: bull's eye—strongly agree; inner ring—agree; middle ring—disagree; and outer ring—strongly disagree.

After everyone has marked all the targets, ask:

- **What would you change about our family if you could?**
- **What are our weakest areas as a family?**
- **How can we strengthen those areas?**

Family Strengths

1. Caring—No lone rangers. Each family member cares about the others.

2. Respectful—Feelings and opinions are respected and can be shared openly.

3. Intelligent—Thirst for knowledge is encouraged and education is highly valued.

4. Steadfast—Consistency of honesty and integrity is encouraged and expected.

5. Physical—Active play and frequent outdoor activities help keep the family healthy.

6. Affectionate—Warmth and understanding is the normal atmosphere of our home.

7. Social—The family has many friends and is involved in the church and community.

8. Responsible—Cooperation and dependability is common.

9. Spiritual—True Christianity is lived out.

10. Motivated—Family members have many interests and tend to be self-starters.

Have someone read aloud Philippians 3:12-14. Say: **Although our family may not be perfect, we can work together to improve life at home.**

Display a 12-month calendar. As a family, set goals for improving family weaknesses. For example, if your family ranks low on "Physical," plan two or three active events over the next few months. Or plan to take up a family sport, such as tennis or basketball. Once your family has set goals, write them on the calendar and display it prominently. Keep track of the family's progress.

Close by joining hands and thanking God for the strengths in your family. Ask God to help make weak areas into strengths.

THE EXTRA MILE

Have family members go through your photo albums and select pictures that highlight good qualities about your family. For instance, they may select pictures that show caring, respect or physical activity. Have family members explain why these qualities are special to them.

SATANISM

PURPOSE: To discuss Satanism and the occult.

MATERIALS: For each family member you'll need a journal, a pencil and a Bible.

PREPARATION: None needed.

GET READY

Have family members number in their journals from one to 12. Read aloud the numbered statements. For each statement, have family members mark A, B or C to reflect their values and feelings. Use this scoring system:

A—I won't do this;

B—I might do this; and

C—I definitely would do this.

Here are the statements:

1. Playing fantasy games
2. Read my horoscope
3. Go to movies about the occult
4. Celebrate Halloween
5. Get involved in occult practices and rituals
6. Have someone tell my fortune or read my palm
7. Play with a Ouija board
8. Use tarot cards
9. Wear my astrological sign
10. Listen to heavy metal music
11. Have a medium get in touch with spirits of the dead for me
12. Make animal sacrifices

GET SET

Assign these scriptures to family members: Leviticus 19:31; Deuteronomy 18:9-14; Isaiah 47:13-15; and Galatians 5:19-21. Have family members each list in their journal the practices that their scripture prohibits. Then ask:
- **Why did God prohibit these practices?**
- **What is God's attitude toward these practices today?**

GO

Say: **Imagine a society where people live to please themselves. Pleasure and gratification are the ideal. Imagine this as a place where the god the people worship requires human sacrifice, and sin is encouraged.**
Ask:
- **What would be some problems with that kind of society?**
- **Why do you feel God forbids us to live that way?**

Pray for those you know are involved in Satanism, witchcraft or the occult. Pray that God would deliver them by Christ's power.

THE EXTRA MILE

Talk to someone from the local police department, school district or other organization who has experience in dealing with the occult. If possible, invite this person to teach your church's teenagers and adults about Satanism and how to help those who may be caught up in it.

CHURCH SMILES

PURPOSE: To celebrate church life.

MATERIALS: You'll need a stack of books and paper.

For each family member you'll need a Bible, a journal, a pencil and a slice of bread.

PREPARATION: None needed.

GET READY

Have family members build a "church" using books, paper and any other materials you have. Once the church is built, have family members collect items that represent what they like about your church. For example, if the people in your church are special, maybe get a photograph of church friends or a magazine picture. Once family members have each collected one or more items, have them each explain their item and place it inside the church they built.

After everyone has shared, ask:
- **What do you like most about our church?**
- **How has our church made a difference in your life?**

GET SET

Form two teams. Have one team look up Ephesians 4:11-16. Have the other team look up Ephesians 4:25-32. Have each team rewrite their passage in their journals, capturing the main ideas and putting them in their own words.

When teams finish, have them each read aloud the original passage and then the rewritten version. Then ask:

- **What's your favorite memory of church?**
- **Who in the church has really helped you at some time? Explain.**

Give each person a slice of bread. Have family members each use their bread to create a symbol for the church. For example, they could make a cross, a heart or a candle. When everyone has finished, have people explain their symbols. Then ask:

- **Why did you choose this symbol?**
- **How does God fit in your symbol?**
- **How would your life be different if you never went to church?**

Thank God for all the positive things about your church each family member shared. Allow each family member to offer a sentence prayer of thanks for the church. Pray that each family member would continue to grow in faith and be involved in the church.

THE EXTRA MILE

Invite members of your church staff and their families to dinner. At the dinner, express your appreciation for them and the work that God accomplishes through them. In the coming weeks, continue to encourage them by sending cards and praying for them.

GIVING THANKS

PURPOSE: To have your family members consider all they're thankful for.

MATERIALS: For each family member you'll need a journal, a pencil and a Bible.

PREPARATION: Thanksgiving dinner would be a great time for the Get Ready section. Follow the meal with the other two sections.

GET READY

On a page in their journal, have family members each take the letters from the word "thanksgiving" and make an acrostic. To form the acrostic, have them choose words that describe what Thanksgiving means to them. For example, for the "T" someone could write "Togetherness."

After everyone has finished, have family members each explain their acrostic.

GET SET

Have everyone kneel in a circle. As a family, read aloud Psalm 105:1-2. Ask:
- **Why is it important to be thankful to God?**
- **What good things has he done for you?**
- **What happens when we tell others what the Lord has done?**

Have the family read aloud 1 Thessalonians 3:9. Ask:

- **Why is it important to thank each other?**
- **Why is it important to thank God for each other?**

Have family members each write their name across the top of a blank page in their journal. Have them each pass their journal to the person on their right. Then have people each write one thing they're thankful for in that person. When everyone has written one thing, have family members pass the journals to the right again, and have them each write one thing for that person. Continue until each person has 12 things about him or her that others are thankful for.

Return the journals to their owners, and allow everyone to read what others wrote.

Have everyone huddle in a circle. Encourage each person to offer a prayer of thanks for God and family members.

THE EXTRA MILE

Pick one or more of these family projects to do during the Thanksgiving season:
- Have the whole family work at a soup kitchen for a few hours on Thanksgiving.
- Give a needy family a complete Thanksgiving dinner. Include a turkey, pie, dressing, gravy, rolls, sweet potatoes and other common Thanksgiving foods.
- Invite someone who'll be alone to have Thanksgiving dinner with your family.

THOSE WACKY PARENTS

PURPOSE: To help kids understand parents.

MATERIALS: You'll need a paper sack for each parent, a piece of paper and one die.

For each family member you'll need a marker, a Bible, a journal and a pencil.

PREPARATION: None needed.

GET READY

Give each parent a paper sack and a marker, and have them each write their name on their sack. Give teenagers each a marker and have them each draw a picture of the parent on that parent's sack. Encourage teenagers to use symbols and words that describe the parent to decorate each parent's sack.

When the sacks are decorated, have the teenagers find five items that best describe each parent. Have them put the items in the appropriate sack. Then have teenagers explain each sack and the items in it. Ask the parents:

● **Does your sack accurately represent you?**

● **In what ways are you misunderstood by your kids?**

GET SET

As a family, play the Understand Me Game on page 147 for about 10 minutes.

After the game, read aloud Ephesians 6:1-3. Have family members each list in their journal five benefits of honoring and obeying your parents. Then ask:

● **What's hard about being a parent?**

● **Why is it important for kids to honor their parents? What can happen if they don't?**

GO

Tell family members they're going to create a poem together. On a piece of paper, write, "Through understanding, our love will grow." Pass the paper to the person on your right. Have that person read what you wrote and add another line. Then have him or her pass the poem to the next person, and repeat the process. Keep going until you have a 12-line poem. Read the poem aloud and ask:

● **How is the way we wrote this poem like the way we grow in love?**

● **Why is it important to understand each other?**

Pray that family members would understand the unique role parents play in the household. Have family members each offer thanks for their parents.

THE EXTRA MILE

Have a "Parent Choice" date! Go out as a family, allowing the parents to decide where you go and what you do.

Understand Me Game

Instructions: This game is used in both the "Those Wacky Parents" devotion and the "Those Wacky Teenagers" devotion. Have each person find a game piece, such as a coin or paper clip. In turn, roll the die and move the appropriate number of spaces on the board. Players may move in any direction.

When a player lands on a space, he or she must read aloud the question, then either answer it or direct it to a parent or teenager—depending on the devotion. For the "Those Wacky Parents" devotion, only parents are allowed to answer questions. For the "Those Wacky Teenagers" devotion, only teenagers are allowed to answer questions.

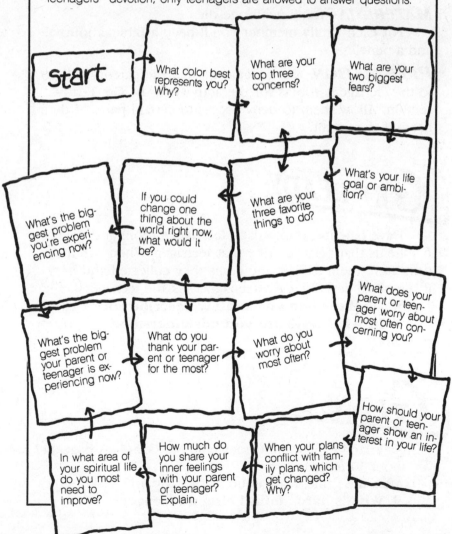

Start

What color best represents you? Why?

What are your top three concerns?

What are your two biggest fears?

What's your life goal or ambition?

What's the biggest problem you're experiencing now?

If you could change one thing about the world right now, what would it be?

What are your three favorite things to do?

What does your parent or teenager worry about most often concerning you?

What's the biggest problem your parent or teenager is experiencing now?

What do you thank your parent or teenager for the most?

What do you worry about most often?

How should your parent or teenager show an interest in your life?

In what area of your spiritual life do you most need to improve?

How much do you share your inner feelings with your parent or teenager? Explain.

When your plans conflict with family plans, which get changed? Why?

THOSE WACKY TEENAGERS

PURPOSE: To help parents understand teenagers.

MATERIALS: You'll need one die.

For each family member you'll need a Bible, a journal and a pencil.

PREPARATION: Warn teenagers that the parents will go to the teenagers' rooms for the activity in the Get Ready section. Allow them to deny access to certain parts of their room if they want.

GET READY

Have parents go into each teenager's room and collect five items that best describe that teenager. When parents return, have them explain the items they collected and how those items describe each teenager. Ask the teenagers:

● **Do these items accurately describe you? Explain.**

● **In what ways are you misunderstood by your parents?**

As a family, play the Understand Me Game on page 147 for about 10 minutes.

After the game, read aloud 1 Timothy 4:12. Ask:

● **What's hard about being a teenager?**

● **How can a teenager practically set an example for believers in speech, life, love, faith and purity?**

Have the teenagers interview the parents about what it was like when they were 15 years old. Have teenagers use the questions below or make up their own.
● What was your height? weight? complexion?
● What did you do for fun?
● How was your school performance?
● What did you do with your friends?
● What activities were you involved in?
● What do you regret the most about those days?
● What did you hope to be?
After the interviews, ask the teenagers:
● **What surprised you about the interviews?**
● **What has changed about being a teenager over the years? What has remained the same?**
Close with prayer by having parents place their hands on their teenagers' shoulders and bless them. Ask God to guide kids to live holy lives and to understand their importance to God and to the family.

THE EXTRA MILE

Have a "Teenager Choice" date! Go out as a family, allowing the teenager to choose where you go and what you'll do.

IMPROVING YOUR SERVE

PURPOSE: To teach family members the importance of serving each other.

MATERIALS: You'll need an old towel, different-color markers, newspapers, a bucket or basin, a sponge or cloth and a clean towel.

For each family member you'll need a journal, a pencil, a different-color marker and a Bible.

PREPARATION: Write the following scripture references in different colors on an old towel or rag: Matthew 20:25-28; Matthew 25:14-21; Luke 16:13; John 12:23-26; 1 Corinthians 12:4-6; and 1 Peter 5:2-4. Fill the bucket or basin with water.

GET READY

Have family members each write their name at the top of a page of their journal. Below their name have them each write 10 ways other family members could serve them. Encourage people to include quick and long projects.

When everyone is finished, have them hand their journal to the person on their left. Family members each must pick one entry from the journal they receive that can be completed in five to 10 minutes, and do that service.

When people have completed their service, ask:
- **What did you enjoy about being served? Why?**
- **What did you dislike about being served? Why?**
- **What did you most enjoy about serving? Why?**
- **What did you dislike about serving? Why?**

GET SET

Give each person a different-color marker. Cover a table with newspapers. On the table, spread the towel on which you wrote scripture references. Assign each family member one or two of the verses. As they read the passages, have them write the characteristics of servants on the towel. Ask:

● **Which servant characteristics are most difficult for you? How can you overcome that difficulty?**

GO

Have the family sit in a circle. Say: **Christ calls us to be servants. In your journal, write one way you can be a better servant to each person in the family.**

Place the bucket of warm water, the sponge and the clean towel in the center of the circle. Read aloud John 13:1-5, 12-17. In turn ask each family member to wash the other family members' feet, following Jesus' example. As they wash, have them tell each person how they'll be a better servant to that person. You go first.

Close with prayer. Pray that God will give each person humility to serve others.

THE EXTRA MILE

Each week, decide together who has served others in an exemplary way, and award the towel from the Get Set section to that person.

SERVING THE LEAST OF THESE

PURPOSE: To focus on the importance and value of serving others.

MATERIALS: You'll need a box of toothpicks and a bag of miniature marshmallows.

For each family member you'll need a journal, a pencil and a Bible.

PREPARATION: None needed.

GET READY

Put the toothpicks and marshmallows on the table. Say: **We're going to build a structure out of these toothpicks and marshmallows. No one may talk while we build. And everyone has to work on the same structure.**

Work together for five to 10 minutes. Then ask:
- **What did you feel as we worked together?**
- **How well did the family work together? How could we improve?**
- **How is this like serving other people?**

GET SET

Have family members think back over the past two days. Ask them each to list in their journals all the people they've come in contact with. Have them include family members, friends, colleagues, acquaintances and people they don't even know, such as store clerks or bank tellers.

Have someone read aloud Matthew 25:31-46. Ask:

● **What does this passage tell us about serving God?**

● **How might your encounters with people during the past two days be similar to the encounters Jesus describes in the passage?**

● **What are ways you could've served those people?**

Read aloud Matthew 25:31-33. Then have family members rewrite the passage using situations they face each day. Ask:

● **How does the updated passage make you feel?**

● **How can the family work together to be more like "the righteous"?**

Read aloud 1 John 3:16-18. Talk about specific ways your family can show Christ's love. Use ideas in "The Extra Mile" box to get started.

Close by praying that you'll grow closer together as a family as you serve God through serving others.

THE EXTRA MILE

Choose one of the following service projects—or another you think of—for your family to do together:

● Volunteer in a nursing home.
● Plant and cultivate a garden for an elderly neighbor.
● Write letters to prison inmates.
● Be tutors in a local literacy program.

THE GIFTS OF CHRISTMAS

PURPOSE: To emphasize the "giving" nature of Christmas.

MATERIALS: You'll need a white tissue or paper, cellophane tape, scissors, a piece of paper, a pencil, Christmas ribbon and a large box.

For each family member you'll need a small cardboard box, a Bible, a wire coat hanger, a journal and a pencil.

PREPARATION: None needed.

GET READY

Give each person a small cardboard box to wrap in white tissue or paper. When all family members each have wrapped their box, have them each write responses to the following things on different sides of their box:
- The best Christmas present I ever received
- The funniest Christmas present I ever received
- The best Christmas present I ever gave
- The most embarrassing present I ever received

Have family members each share what they wrote. Ask:
- **Why is Christmas an important time?**
- **Why do we give gifts at Christmas?**

GET SET

Ask a family member to read aloud Matthew 1:18—2:13

and Luke 2:1-20. Whenever someone hears a gift mentioned in the text, have him or her interrupt the reading and explain the gift. Write down all the gifts. Then ask:

- **In what way was Jesus a gift to the world?**
- **What gifts can we give Jesus this Christmas?**

Give people each a wire hanger and some ribbon. Have them each design a symbol of a gift they can give Jesus. For example, someone might design a harp with ribbon as strings to symbolize a spirit of joy.

Have family members each explain their designs. Then say: **Seeing presents wrapped and under the tree reminds us of the gifts we give each other. Let's wrap our symbolic gifts as a reminder to us of the one who deserves our greatest gifts and adoration.**

Put all the symbols in a large box. As a family, wrap the box using white tissue or paper. Decorate the outside of the box with ribbon and each person's name. Close by singing your family's favorite Christmas carols.

THE EXTRA MILE

Put the decorated box under your Christmas tree or in another prominent place in your house. Open that gift first this Christmas.

TOPICAL INDEX